the BASS PLAYER'S HANDBOOK

GREG MOOTER

Berklee Media

Associate Vice President: Dave Kusek
Director of Content: Debbie Cavalier
Marketing Manager: Jennifer Rassler
Senior Graphic Designer: David Ehlers

Berklee Press

Senior Writer/Editor: Jonathan Feist
Writer/Editor: Susan Gedutis
Production Manager: Shawn Girsberger

ISBN 0-634-02300-4

1140 Boylston Street
Boston, MA 02215-3693 USA
(617) 747-2146

Visit Berklee Press Online at
www.berkleepress.com

DISTRIBUTED BY

HAL•LEONARD®
CORPORATION
7777 W. BLUEMOUND RD. P.O. BOX 13819
MILWAUKEE, WISCONSIN 53213

Visit Hal Leonard Online at
www.halleonard.com

Contents

Illustrations

Acknowledgments

Special thanks to technicians David Gage, Peter Kyvelos, Lenny Harlos, and Wolf Ginandes. To luthiers Kai Arvi, Albey Balgochian, Mike Pedulla, and Vinnie Fodera. For their physical guidance, to Dr. Charles De Cecca, Dr. Wayne Wescott, Arthur Brodie, and Dr. Richard Norris. To teachers Lou Lausche, John Neves, Steve Swallow, Rich Appleman, John Repucci, Charlie Banacos, and David Cobb.

Extra special thanks to Whit Browne, for his technical assistance, wonderful photos, and numerous early morning clinics. To Joe Santerre, for his tasteful electric poses. To Joe Carson, for his excellent stretch poses. To Marilyn Bone Kloss, for her editorial assistance.

To my father, Paul, and my brother, John, for allowing one more musician in the family. And to my wife, Mil, for tolerating my personality without complaint.

Preface

This book is a guide for contemporary bassists in their quest for information related to their instrument. It is presented to clarify ideas and to reinforce musicianship. I have collected what I believe to be vital information all bassists need know about their instrument's origin, construction, and workings. In addition, I outline some essential ideas on proper fingering concepts, tone production, good practice habits, and the retention of good physical health related to playing.

This book is a start for the student and a reminder for the professional. In no way is it meant to be a substitute for a long-standing relationship with a fine teacher and detailed reading of the many volumes of information available on the subject matter. Regarding performance skills, the knowledge gained from an experienced teacher far surpasses that gained from any text. This book is intended as a supplement to the performance skills imparted by a professional, skilled instructor. Technical skills and musicianship cannot be learned from paper, only from the instrument.

Introduction

Within this text, I make numerous references to specific pitches. The system I use is that of the standard means of numbering the pitches on a piano keyboard.

I also make numerous references to the right and left hands. I do not wish to further depress my left-handed friends, as they have been depressed by society for countless centuries, but since the majority of the population is right handed, my references assume right-handedness. The right hand is the touch, bow holding, or articulating hand, and the left hand is the work, or note-closing hand.

To simplify the numerous varieties of available stringed bass instruments, this book references them as two types: electric and double. *Electric* includes all instruments held in the fashion of the guitar, including, bass guitar, acoustic bass guitar, baritone guitar, and similar instruments. An instrument need not be "electric" to be included in this category; any bass instrument shaped and sized similar to a long-scale electric bass is referred to as "electric." *Double* includes the double bass, stick-style basses, electric acoustic instruments, and other instruments of similar shape and size. All

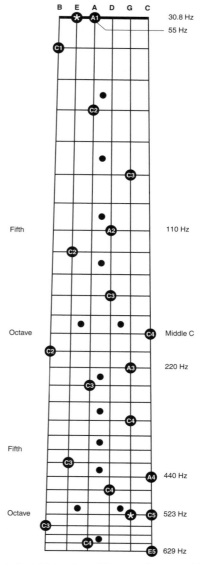

Fig. I.1. 6-String Bass Pitch Numbering Table.
★★Range of a 2-octave 4-string bass.

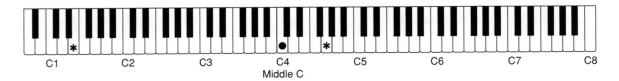

*Fig. I.2. Keyboard Pitch Numbering Table. **Range of a 2-octave 4-string bass.*

instruments played upright, or vertically, are referred to as "double." There are, of course, some instruments that seem to cross between the two categories. An electric acoustic has electronic controls, and an acoustic bass guitar may have none. When attempting to reference specific instruments to the information contained herein, let common sense be your guide.

A list of bass methods and supplemental bass literature is included in the Resources section. I am by no means suggesting that all readers should go out and purchase any or all of these books to better themselves musically, but an adequate personal library of bass music would include many of these volumes. It is my intention to provide guidance and supplemental material to aspiring bassists and hungry professionals. The lists of bass books, music, and studies will be of most use to students who are attempting study without the aid of an instructor, for much, or all, of these materials would surely be recommended to students by most knowledgeable instructors.

CHAPTER 1
Roots

Double

The double bass, as we know it today, has taken on enormous changes since its first ancestors appeared at around 1200 or so. Large-sized *gigues* (see fig. 1.1) produced during this time period performed the bass function in the day's popular music, but it is difficult to draw a direct relationship from the gigue to the double bass. There is very little physical evidence remaining of the early bass instruments, aside from some occasional sketches, so the majority of the structural details of these instruments will never be known.

The early bass instruments were of a wide variety of shapes and sizes. The development and manufacture of bass function instruments appears to have been haphazard, at best, until around 1600, when the viol da gamba appeared (see fig. 1.2). This instrument had five or six strings, usually tuned in fifths, and had *c* holes on its face. From written accounts, it appears that there was not a standard size, as historical accounts list varying sized instruments. Around this same time in Germany, bass instruments began to appear in the shape of the viol, while it appears that the Italians of this period preferred the violin shape, which included an arched back. These early double basses closely resemble modern double basses, and many of them still survive in collections and museums. The early German and Italian double basses estab-

Fig. 1.1. Grosse Gigue

Fig. 1.2. Viol da Gamba

lished the general sizes and shapes that live on today. They also included *f* holes on their fronts, like other members of the violin family.

An Italian bass maker, Gasparo da Salo (1540–1609), was making instruments at this time, some of which still exist. It is known that he made a 3-stringed bass used two centuries later by Domenico Dragonetti (1763–1846). Dragonetti is the grandfather of all famous bass characters! He was known to have amazing chops and was quite a showman. He would often stand at the front of the orchestra and play fancy lines to show off during the performance. If there was an area of rest in his part, he would often look over to the player beside him and play his part, in the correct octave . . . it was usually a violin part! He was a friend to Beethoven, and some historians believe that some of Beethoven's parts were written with Dragonetti in mind as the principal player. He was the Jaco of his time!

The early double basses were even more diverse than electric basses are today. Variations in size, shape, angling, arching, number of strings, and tuning are just some that were encountered. String length, in particular, varied to a much greater extent on early instruments than is the case today. These sometimes large variations would be quite difficult for the modern-day bassist to deal with. In the 1600–1800s, travel was slow and communication was slow. Musicians didn't travel a great deal. A bass player might spend his entire life in one town, so he wouldn't be exposed to these variations; he would only know his instrument or those made by local luthiers. The large variations did not affect the average player. In addition, there were no CDs! Music was communicated by ear and by the written part, so you couldn't get excited about Dragonetti unless he came to your town for a concert. Most bass players didn't even know who Dragonetti was, let alone what kind of bass he played and what brand of strings he used.

Many of these variations have carried through to today's instruments, but usually to a much smaller degree. Today, we have size standards, but there also continues to exist size variations from one instrument brand to another, and even within instruments made by the same luthier or company. This, of course, includes string length, which is probably the variable of most concern to the player, since it directly affects physical technique.

Most modern-day basses are 4-stringed and tuned in fourths. In the early days, many 5-stringed instruments were produced, and numerous tunings were utilized, which varied the interval as well as the pitches of the open strings. As mentioned above, it is also known that Dragonetti played a 3-stringed bass, tuned in fifths. The legendary sound of this instrument is well documented, and many believe that the presence of just three strings allowed Dragonetti extra power and volume because the string pressure exerted on the instrument was lessened.

Today's instruments include all of the surviving classic instruments of the last two centuries, many high-quality newer instruments made by present-day luthiers, factory-made plywood instruments, and everything in between. It is this large array of instruments, the time span involved with their manufacture, and the sheer size of the double bass that account, in most part, for the variations available from instrument to instrument. Most other modern-day instruments are built much more closely to strict physical standards. It sure makes being a double bassist interesting.

Early strings were made of animal gut, and in fact, some of the early bass instruments even featured gut frets. Playing on gut strings was an arduous task for our predecessors. The strings were much fatter than modern-day metal strings. It was very difficult to keep them in tune, as they were continuously stretching and decomposing. In addition, the gut material did not sound clearly in the very low register—not good for a bass!

Metal strings were introduced in the early 1900s, and the gut string problems were solved, for the most part. Many players switched to the thinner, clearer sounding metal strings, as long as their instrument could handle the extra tension these strings exerted. Others, who preferred the traditional gut sound and feel, were offered metal-wrapped A and E gut strings. The metal wrapping allowed the thickness of these lower strings to be reduced greatly and the clarity of pitch to be enhanced.

Of course, bass bows have developed and changed along with the double bass. Early bows were an arched stick with some hair strung on it, kind of like a mini archer's bow with hair instead of string. As the carving of basses developed, the carving of bows also developed. In time, there emerged two standard bows: German and French (see fig. 2.5).

Dragonetti, an Italian, played on what was then called an *Italian* bow, which he developed. It was adopted and further developed by the Germans, in particular Franz Simandl (1840–1912), and so this style of bow has come to be called the *German* bow. It is held in an underhanded fashion.

Another Italian, Giovanni Bottesini (1821–1889), preferred the style of bow we now call the *French*. He was another of our famous bass characters and was quite a flamboyant player. He incorporated much use of harmonics in his fancy melodic style of playing. The French bow came after the German. It is held in an overhand fashion, like the other bows of the violin family.

The double bass and its bows and strings have taken on general standards, but within these standards are endless subtle variables and variations. Many of these variables and variations are meant to accommodate individual players' physical requirements. Others are designed to produce some degree of musical or tonal variation. In all cases, modern-day double bassists must educate themselves to the variations and variables available in today's instruments, so that they can most closely meet their specific physical and musical needs.

Electric

It would be useful, at this point, to define the electric bass. Generally speaking, an electric bass is a non-acoustic instrument with a size and shape slightly larger than a conventional electric guitar. It has a harmonic range similar to that of the double bass, and in fact, the tuning is generally the same. Although some instruments have hollow bodies, they are not generally meant to be played without amplification. Originally, it was the magnetic pickup, not the body size and shape, that was the defining factor in differentiating the early electrics from the "electric acoustics." This original pickup design has been modified to include numerous other pickup types in more recent years.

Prior to 1938, popular music was getting louder and louder. Unlike an orchestra, dance bands had but one bass player, and it was very difficult for the bass player to compete with a full horn section and a set of drums. Microphones were used to amplify the double bass, but 1930's technology left much to be desired from amplification systems. Early amplification systems did a poor job of picking up the bass without feedback, and the tone was muddy, at best.

There were many great bass players working at this time, but performing night after night without being able to clearly hear oneself left many of the "everyday" players in the dust. Unless the rest of the band was sensitive to the bass player's volume constraints, performing was often a frustrating experience.

During this period, a number of instrument companies were experimenting with electric/acoustic and quasi-electric basses. The Vega Company of Boston, Massachusetts built a slim stick type bass. Gibson of Kalamazoo, Michigan built several acoustic/electric basses that were shaped similarly to their line of hollow-body electric guitars, only king size.

At this time, there were also other luthiers and performers building instruments that were not intended for public distribution.

It was in 1935 that the Rickenbacker Company built what is generally accepted as the first prototype electric bass (see fig. 1.3). The primary idea behind this instrument was easy and clear amplification. The instrument's shape resembled a modern-day stick-type bass. A second, more refined, instrument was produced in 1938.

Both instruments had fingerboards that were arched and fretless like that of a double bass. Both versions featured pegs (tuners) similar to those of a double bass, and the feel of the neck was also made to mimic the feel of a double bass. But the string length was more like a Fender, and these instruments had volume and tone controls. They also had magnetic pickups. The prototype instruments used gut strings with metal wrapping on them above the pickups, creating a signal that could be sensed by the magnetic pickups.

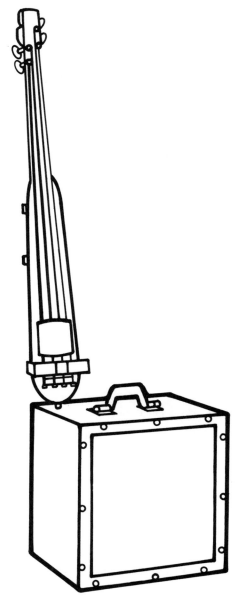

Bassists played the 1935 model by standing just behind the amplifier and resting the endpin of the bass on top of it. The 1938 model had a separate stand, or it could be balanced on the floor. In either case, the instrument stood upright, as does the double bass. These bass instruments were mutants of the double bass, but they resembled the electric bass that was to come only in that they utilized magnetic pickups, which were one of the hallmarks of the early electric bass.

Today, there are a number of electric/acoustic instruments available, most of which resemble the early Rickenbacker design. These instruments have the feel of a double bass, and many sound much like an amplified double bass. For convenience, a number of models can be collapsed, making long distance travel quite accessible. Of course, since they are electric, they all contain various amounts of electronics for sound reproduction.

Fig. 1.3. Rickenbacker's Electro Bass Viol (1935)

In 1940, Vernon Alley became Lionel Hampton's bass player. He played with Lionel's band from 1940–43. During this time he occasionally performed on one of these Rickenbacker prototype electric basses at Hampton's request.

Alley had been a disc jockey in the San Francisco area around this time and was a local "celebrity." He can be seen performing on the prototype bass in the film clip "Susan Hayward's Hit Parade of 1943" (in some catalogs, called "Change of Heart"). He can also be heard performing on the bass with the Lionel Hampton Big Band on the track "Altitude," which is on the album collection *The Complete Lionel Hampton 1937–1941*.

After the conclusion of World War II, there was great exuberance in the USA. Big bands were as popular and loud as ever. All of the GIs returned to the States looking to return to their jobs or establish new ones. Musicians found plenty of work, but as is still the case today, there was a surplus of guitar players. Many guitar players looked to playing the bass in order to secure enough work to make a living, but few wanted to alter their guitar technique by mastering the much larger and fretless double bass. These late 1940s guitar players were to become the first electric bassists in the early 1950s. The aforementioned prototype bass was not considered a viable choice of instrument by these guitar players, as they considered it too large and unruly.

In 1947, an inventor named Everett Hull placed a transducer inside a double bass by means of an extended endpin or peg. Soon thereafter, the Ampeg (amplified peg) company was born. This company became an innovator in amplification systems, and double bass players took another step forward. But this device did not help to create the electric bass, and guitar players were not impressed.

In the meantime, Leo Fender had become a leader in the field of electric guitar production. Now, many of his customers were asking him, and other luthiers associated with him, to develop a bass instrument that they could play in a similar fashion as the guitar.

Fender worked on designs in the late 1940s and early 1950s, and in late 1951, the Fender Precision Bass was born. Fender had modified the Broadcaster Guitar and created the first electric bass guitar.

The Precision Bass was a wonderful blend of the guitar and the double bass. It had four strings, was tuned like the double bass and the lowest four strings of a guitar, and could function musically like its father. Its overall size and string length was a cross between double bass and electric guitar. It could be played in a similar fashion to the electric guitar, was fretted, and was amplified, like its mother.

Fig. 1.4. Fender Precision Bass (1951). Courtesy of Backbeat Books.

The cutaway shape was created for weight and balance. This shape has become one of the signatures of a Fender. The performer could pluck the strings with a pick, the fingers, or the thumb; after all, no one had a clue as to where this instrument was going.

The instrument allowed the bassist to play with ease and afforded precision of intonation through the use of frets, thus the name Precision Bass. Leo Fender once stated that players could even do dance steps while performing, enhancing many pop-style performances.

Most double bassists of this time were still somewhat dissatisfied with their lack of volume control but were not interested in playing an instrument shaped like a guitar. In fact, this dislike of the electric bass by most double bassists kept them from the electric bass for many years. From 1951 until around 1973 or so, there was a division between double bassists and electric bassists, who were considered to be playing "toys." This "toy" attitude also extended to many other instrumentalists, and in fact, was well founded, in many cases. When the electric bass was young, few players took it seriously. Technique was haphazard, at best. There was no literature specifically written for the instrument. The sound could never be described as natural, which is what the double bass players were looking for. "Serious" musicians avoided it like the plague.

It was the popular music of the late 1950s, and more so the 1960s, that eventually attracted some talented players to the instrument. These electric bassists did not have a predetermined point of view as to what a bass was, but had to literally create it as their musical needs demanded. A little later, it was the pioneer players of the 1960s and 1970s who accounted for the influx of virtuoso players at present. Of course, advances in technology and changing musical styles also account for the present-day popularity of the electric bass.

In 1953, Monk Montgomery, a double bassist, joined the Lionel Hampton Band (see fig. 1.5). Hampton wanted the electric sound and instructed Montgomery to buy a Fender in order to hold down the gig. Monk did so, and soon became the first to record on the electric bass, as Hampton's band recorded later that year. The original album release was called *He Swings the Most*, but now it is available as a reissue entitled *Lionel Hampton's Paris All Stars*. This is a live album made in a large hall, and it is a great representation of the classic sound of the early electric bass.

Also in 1953, Gibson introduced the EB1. It was a smaller instrument than the Fender and had the characteristic Gibson horns along with the characteristic deep tone.

By 1956, there were many electric basses on the market, and the instrument was becoming very popular with rock and roll bands. Most of the players, however, were still originally guitar players. This fact was instrumental in the Dan Electro company's release of the first 6-string electric bass. It was tuned like a guitar but down an octave to facilitate its use by guitarists. The strings were spaced closer than was the case with the Fender, and most players used a pick to perform on it.

Fig. 1.5. Monk and Wes Montgomery. Photo by Veryl Oakland, reprinted with permission.

The following year, the Rickenbacker Company introduced its first electric basses (see fig. 1.6). They featured the classic Rickenbacker shape we know today and the first neck-through-body design.

In 1959, as the electric bass achieved more acceptance in the music community, Fender introduced its Jazz Bass (see fig. 1.7). The two pickups and two tone controls allowed the performer a wider range of sounds. It also had a more tapered neck facilitating ease of performance with the left hand.

Fender came out with its version of the 6-string three years later; it was tuned like the Dan Electro. By this time, however, more and more electric bassists were first generation electric players, not converted double bassists or guitar players, and the Fender 6-string never gained popular acceptance. Today, most of these instruments reside in the closets of elderly guitar players.

In 1964, Fender began production of a 5-string instrument. It was tuned like the conventional electric bass with the addition of a high C string. This instrument was a little ahead of its time and was not highly accepted at this time.

It was also around this time that Ampeg began marketing its line of electric/acoustic basses. Among their products was the Baby Bass. Some double bassists liked this instrument, as it was easy to transport and amplify, and felt similar to a double bass. But by this time, deep lines had been drawn, and most double bassists insisted upon staying with their acoustic instruments. Electric players, for the most part, were not interested in converting to a larger instrument with no frets.

Fig. 1.6. Rickenbacker Electric Bass (1957)

Fig. 1.7. Fender Jazz Bass (1964).
Courtesy of Backbeat Books.

Fender, in the hopes of capitalizing on the younger market of early teens, introduced a short-scale electric bass in 1966. Fender now had scales of 30, 32, and 34 inches, thus allowing small and large players the ability to reach all of the notes with ease. It was generally believed that the tone of the shorter scale instruments was inferior to the long scale Precision and Jazz Basses.

By this time, the "Rotosound" sound was quite popular in England and spreading elsewhere rapidly. Players such as Chris Squire and John Paul Jones were spreading the sound around the globe. The Rotosound Company was now marketing its products internationally, and the electric bassist suddenly had a whole new sound. Up until this time, most strings were flat wound and of a relative heavy gauge. It was not uncommon for a G string to be 50 to 60 gauge. Rotosound produced a round-wound string with a variety of gauges. The Jazz Bass RS66 set of the mid 1960s was the most popular. These strings produced a characteristic metallic growling sound made popular by John Entwistle of The Who, and they paved the way for the wide variety of strings available today.

At this same time, amplification was also improving. As the market widened, companies improved their products. Solid state was now available, and large speaker systems were commonplace.

By 1970, the electric bass was being used in jazz, and Fender produced the first fretless electric as a Jazz Bass. It had a rosewood fingerboard but was a classic Jazz Bass otherwise. This instrument allowed many electric bassists to obtain jazz gigs.

In 1976, Kramer introduced a bass with an aluminum neck. The aluminum was intended to stabilize the neck in performance and during weather changes. In addition, the solid construction helped the instrument's sustain. Later that year, the Alembic company was born with the help of The Grateful Dead. Alembic was the first large company to specialize in high-quality customized instruments.

The year 1979 saw the introduction of the Steinberger Bass (see fig. 1.8). It was constructed of molded plastic and had no machines. Many people called it the "headless" bass. By this time, active electronics were commonplace, and many new pickup designs were available.

Stringed instruments have been made primarily of wood for hundreds of years. Both the Kramer, and more so, the Steinberger, gained popular acceptance, but the great majority of electric bassists preferred the more traditional wood instrument. In later years, the Modulus, featuring graphite construction, was also highly accepted, possibly due to the fact that the graphite looks and feels a lot like ebony. The feel and look of wood is a tradition that has not been lost.

By 1986, the market was flooded with just about any style of bass you would like to pay for, and 5- and 6-string instruments as we know them today were widely available. The 5-string instruments were of the high C or low B varieties, the 6-string was a combination of the two. Also, by this time, Roland had introduced the MIDI Bass Guitar Synthesizer; this type of instrument continues to develop today. The electronic configuration of an electric bass was limited only by the buyer's imagination.

Throughout the 1990s, companies continued to add and subtract strings. Instrument size and shape varied greatly. At present, there may appear to be no standardization in the construction of the electric bass, and when one considers all of the musical styles and playing techniques in vogue, it becomes clear why this is so. Modern day players are required to tap, slap, rock out, funk it up, do a little Motown, jazz it, and of course, solo. In addition, the electric bass has always been a "street instrument." Many players learn their craft on the job, at the jam session, or on the street corner. All of these facts help to account for the wide variety of instrument styles demanded by the diverse selection of performers with their varying needs and desires. Performers purchase instruments that suit their needs, and their needs are boundless.

The electric bass is still an infant, by historical standards. First marketed in 1952, it has barely achieved a half-century of tradition. What tradition it has achieved is due primarily to the musical styles of the latter part of the twentieth century and the whims of the players. Where it will go next is anyone's guess.

Fig. 1.8. Steinberger Electric Bass. Photo courtesy of Gibson Musical Instruments.

CHAPTER 2

Instrument Construction

Double

Double basses available today can be categorized as either *carved* or *plywood*. Some plywood basses have high-quality wood laminated on the outer surfaces, so as to give the look of a carved instrument. There are also many instruments available that combine a carved top with an otherwise plywood or laminated instrument. Instruments are also occasionally constructed of fiberglass and aluminum for special "heavy duty" work.

Plywood is not synonymous with cheap nor is carved always high quality. However, plywood instruments are generally less expensive than carved. A fine instrument can only be found through the careful attention of the bassist to the playability and the sound of each instrument auditioned. Each player brings his own experiences to the judgment of an instrument. Many players prefer a plywood instrument, as it will withstand the abuses of traveling from place to place much better than a carved instrument will. Be aware that if the bass is going to be amplified, its acoustic sound can be altered considerably depending on the type of amplification used. In any case, well-seasoned wood must be used to minimize shrinkage after construction.

Instrument shapes vary greatly, due mainly to the facts that there are thousands of builders, each with their own twist on appearances, and that so many older instruments are still available, each with its own characteristic shape. The sheer size of the instrument makes each shape variation very noticeable to the eye. Newer instruments adhere more closely to a general shape. In older instruments, the lack of standardization, lack of good communication, local need for instruments, and local need for work all contributed to the diverse shapes.

It is almost pointless to have a discussion related to instrument size, considering the countless varieties that exist. Naturally, factory-built instruments adhere to a set of standards, but these standards flex from company to company. Standard sizes do exist on paper, but they are not a reality in practice. Many of the nicest instruments are built for a specific owner to specifications divergent from the standards. It is best for us to think of the standards as guidelines.

We commonly consider many instruments to be 7/8 and 5/8 sizes. These sizes, in reality, are mutant sizes and are personalized variations on the standard sizes.

C. Carving the inside back

A. Front, inside

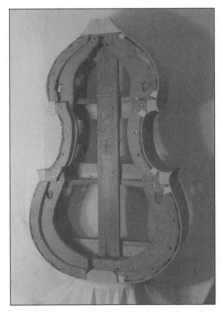

B. Ribs, corner blocks, neck block and
   end pin block

D. Carving the top

Fig. 2.1. In the Luthier's Shop

E. Gluing on the back

G. The finished front

F. The neck

H. Inside, without the front

Fig. 2.1. In the Luthier's Shop (continued)

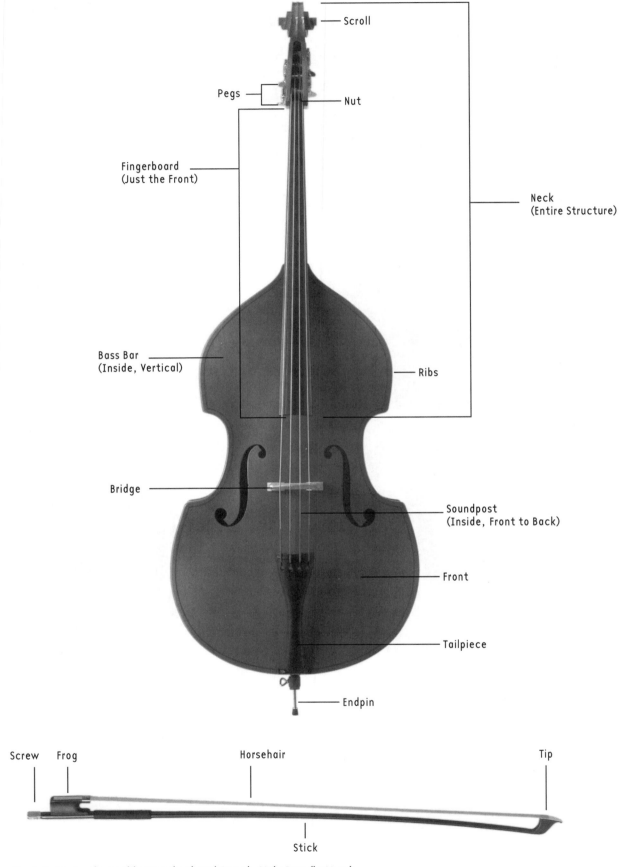

Scroll

Pegs — Nut

Fingerboard
(Just the Front)

Neck
(Entire Structure)

Bass Bar
(Inside, Vertical)

Ribs

Bridge

Soundpost
(Inside, Front to Back)

Front

Tailpiece

Endpin

Screw   Frog   Horsehair   Tip

Stick

Fig. 2.2. Parts of a Double Bass (top) and French-Style Bow (bottom)

Standard Measurements for Standard-Sized Double Basses
(in millimeters)

	4/4	3/4	1/2	1/4
Body Length	1160	1110	1020	940
Fingerboard Length	890	850	780	730
String Length	1100	1060	975	900
Tailpiece Length	350	340	310	290
Widest Point on Front	680	650	600	557

Fig. 2.3. Standard Measurements for Standard-Sized Double Basses. As designated by the Music Educator's National Conference.

Front

The *front* (also called the "top" or "belly") is usually made of spruce, fir, or fine-quality pine. These are elastic woods and have been found to vibrate nicely. It is most common for the top to be two pieces of wood from the same tree, glued together in the center so as to give the appearance that it is a single board. The center of the front is carved slightly thicker, supporting the arch and facilitating a secure and perfect fit of the two pieces.

Joint

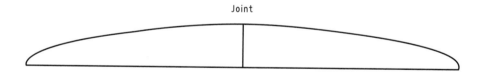

Fig. 2.4. Cross Section of the Front

The instrument maker must carefully carve the pieces to exact proportions for a perfect fit. It is generally agreed that the builder will devote his deepest attention to the proper shaping and grading of this part of the instrument.

Upon completion of the front, the *f* holes are marked and cut. The center slash in the *f* holes marks the horizontal plane at which the bridge will be located. These holes allow for the passage of air to and from the inside of the instrument. The exact shape of the holes varies from instrument to instrument, but it is generally believed that the *f* shape aids the tone of bowed instruments.

Back

The *back* is said to be *flat* or *round* and is made of two or more pieces or wood. A *round-backed* instrument is actually shaped in an arch. Maple is the predominant construction wood of choice, but other nicely grained hard and fruitwoods have been used with good success. The *flat-back* instrument requires a number of crossbraces, but the arched back better supports itself and is reinforced only at the center by small cleats.

As with the top, much care must be taken to carve the back to perfect proportions, so as to create a perfect fit and minimize stress under adverse conditions. It is generally believed that the round-backed instrument reacts more favorably to weather changes. In terms of sound, both are equally loved by their owners.

Ribs

The *ribs*, or *sides*, are also traditionally made of maple. The boards are cut to the proper lengths, shaped by using a heat treatment, and fitted and glued together. Here, as with all of the other parts, proper thickness must be carefully calibrated.

The ribs hold the front and back together, but there are other theoretical functions. It is obvious that the sides help to contain the air mass within the instrument. It is also believed that they aid in transmitting the sound from the front to the back, so as to generate proper instrument vibration.

Blocks are placed within the body of the instrument to lend support at the four corners and at the neck and tailpiece. These are usually made of pine or spruce and must be fitted to give even support.

Bass Bar

The *bass bar* is a supporting piece of spruce or pine that is fitted and glued to the underside of the front. Its location is vertical along the front, lengthwise passing under the left foot of the bridge.

The function of this piece is twofold. Its presence lends support to the top, which receives much pressure from the tension of the strings. It also disperses the sound received from the bridge over the entire front.

The bass bar must be in proportion to the instrument. Altering its size and shape will affect the sound of the instrument.

Soundpost

The *soundpost* is a ¾-inch diameter pine dowel with its grain running lengthwise. It is fitted between the top and the back at about a thumb's width distance below the right foot of the bridge. It must fit snugly into place, being neither too tight nor too loose, fitting perfectly to the contours of the front and back.

The soundpost supports the top under the pressure of the strings. It also reduces excessive movement of the top while transmitting the sound from the top to the back. This allows the top and back to vibrate in tandem.

Bridge

The *bridge* is traditionally fashioned out of fine maple. As previously mentioned, its location is determined by the cuts in the *f* holes. Although this location can be altered to change the scale of the instrument, the builder will always recommend not to do so. This location is determined as part of the complicated calibrations needed in building a bass.

The bridge must be contoured, or arched, to fit the fingerboard. This semi-round shape is necessary to allow the bowing of the inner strings one at a time. Bridge thickness and height must also be matched to each specific instrument.

It is possible to install adjusters, or rollers, to the bridge to allow small action adjustments necessary to accommodate seasonal changes in the instrument. These adjustors may also aid players who perform varied styles of music. Jazz or pop players, not incorporating arco in their playing, often like the bridge lower than do orchestral players, who need a certain height to accommodate the wider swing of a bowed string. Players using a pickup system may also set the bridge lower, as they are able to play more gently and still be heard by use of the volume control.

Neck

The *neck* is traditionally made of maple. Most often, a single piece of wood is used to fashion the neck and scroll, as a joint in the connection area of the two would create a weak spot where there is much string tension. The neck length helps determine the string scale of the instrument and must be in proportion with all other measurements.

Fingerboard

Quality *fingerboards* are made of ebony. Less expensive instruments often use stained maple to simulate ebony, but these fingerboards quickly develop ruts from the wear caused by the pressure of the vibrating strings against them. Even ebony fingerboards will rut in time, and may need to be planed and dressed by a craftsman to regain their proper surface shape. Plywood basses are often fitted with rosewood fingerboards to save expense.

There is much intricate detailing necessary to shape the fingerboard so that it functions properly and feels comfortable. Without proper shape, a fingerboard will cause string buzzing and uneven pitch levels. As mentioned earlier, the bridge and fingerboard contours must be matched.

Scroll

The *scroll* (also called "scrollbox" or "pegbox") sits atop the neck. This structure has a hollowed out inner chamber where the strings attach to the pegs. It is often a characteristically carved shape, and holds the pegs (see below). As stated above, the scroll and neck should be carved from a single piece of wood to aid in overall stability under the pressures of string tension, performance, and instrument transporting.

Pegs

The *pegs* are the mechanisms to which the strings are attached for tightening. Modern pegs are no longer literally pegs, but the term remains in use for what is better termed the *tuning machines*. These machines consist of a slotted key that fits into a wheel, which is attached to a shaft upon which the strings wrap. The shaft is fitted through holes in the sides of the scroll, and the entire mechanism is attached to a plate that is screwed onto the side of the scrollbox. Most tuning keys are attached to the sides of the scroll in groups of two, but they can also be attached separately. Quality machines are made of brass or bronze. The peg shaft is usually brass or bronze, but many older instruments that still retain their original machines have ebony peg shafts. Some older plywood or "assembly line" carved instruments have maple shafts, stained black to appear as ebony.

Endpin

The *endpin* is located at the bottom of the instrument. High quality endpins are made of steel and are adjustable to allow the player to adjust the height of the bass. The endpin is fitted into an ebony sleeve, which in turn is fitted into the bottom of the instrument.

Tailpiece

The *tailpiece* is of carved ebony, or other quality hardwood, and is best attached to the endpin fitting by use of heavy wire. Its purpose is to anchor the strings below the bridge.

Nut

The *nut* is located at the top end of the fingerboard and is generally carved of ebony. The grooves in it must be cut to hold the strings but not smother them in a slit that is too deep. Some instruments have a "false nut" installed below the location of the original nut, which in effect, shortens the instrument scale without moving the bridge.

Finish

Oil-based finish is used to protect the wood and to add color, which enhances the beauty of the wood. Spirit-based varnishes tend to chip and are less desirable for use as a finish on a fine instrument.

Strings

There are a number of brands and types of strings available today, but they generally fall into three types: gut, soft core wound, and steel core wound.

The most traditional bass strings are made of gut. Some gut type strings are currently being made of nylon. In either case, the lower strings are usually wound with plated copper wire.

Soft or rope-core strings are the choice of most orchestral players, as these strings produce a beautiful bowed sound. The center core of these strings is wrapped with metal, usually chromium or aluminum.

Steel core strings are often the choice of jazz players. The 100-percent metal construction gives a strong attack to the pizzicato, and these strings often emit a wonderful growl. A variety of metals are used to form the wrapping.

Bows

As discussed in chapter 1, bows have evolved greatly through the centuries, and today there are two types in general use: French and German.

The bow is composed of a stick, which has a frog and screw at one end and a tip at the other (see fig. 2.2). Horsehair is strung from the frog to the tip.

The *frog* holds the hair at the desired distance away from the stick, aids in the gripping of the bow, and allows for the tension of the hair to be altered by means of the screw. Frogs are made of ebony, and quite often they have beautiful inlay on them. The frog must be properly fitted

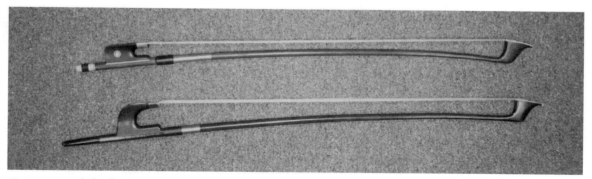

Fig. 2.5. French (top) and German (bottom) Bows

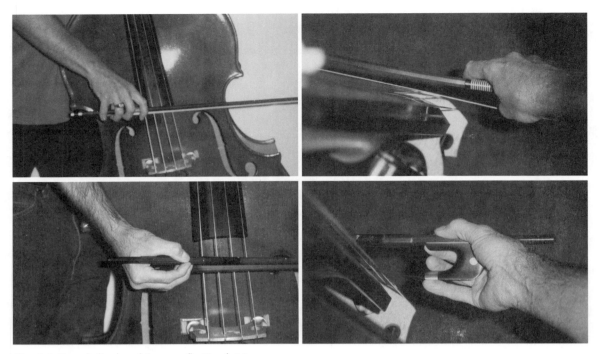

Fig. 2.6. French (top) and German (bottom) Grips

to the stick so as to allow smooth movement when the hairs are tightened. The screw that tightens the frog passes into the stick and attaches by means of an eyelet screw.

The *point* or *tip* is the outer end of the bow where the hairs attach. Small amounts of weight can be added within the tip to adjust the overall balance of the bow to suit the individual player. Weight can also be added in the wrapping at the frog.

The *sticks* of quality bows are made of Pernambuco. There are, however, a number of less expensive woods used today, and student models are made of fiberglass. The most important attribute of the stick is its flexibility. Care should be taken not to overtighten or forget to loosen the hairs after playing, as in time, this will adversely affect the flexibility of the stick.

The coarse texture of the horsehair, which allows it to grab the string and cause vibration, deteriorates over time and with prolonged use, and individual hairs break from time to time during normal use. Consequently, it is necessary to have the hair replaced at regular intervals. There are specialists who do this work in most cities, and when you find one you like, make a friend. Rehairing should be done annually, at least, or you are not playing enough!

Accessories

• E-String Extension

There is much music written for the double bass that goes below E1. Since this is the lowest note on the conventional 4-stringed instrument, extensions are often added to the E string that extend the range down to C1. Adding an extension requires modifications to the scroll area in order to accommodate the extension fingerboard and the required longer string.

The *keyed extension* features a set of flute-like keys that operate the note stops. The original model is the Fawcett E-String Extension. Each extension must be tailored to work with the string scale of the specific instrument it is intended to fit. The inventor and builder, Ronald Prentice, has retired. There are many similar models available for addition to any double bass.

The *fingered extension* has no keys, but rather, the notes are stopped with the fingers in the usual manner. It is cumbersome to reach these notes, at times, since they are located up the scroll, so technique modification and practice will be required. Note stops (or gates) and frets may be added to this type of extension, and some players will occasionally use a capo to establish the lowest note needed, if it is above open C1. In any case, the addition of an E-string extension is a job for an experienced technician.

• Rosin

Rosin is a product of tree sap, generally oak. Most fine rosins, such as Carlsson, Pops, and Nyman Hartts, are made in Sweden.

Different brands of rosin vary in their texture and stickiness. It is this stickiness, or glue-like quality, that allows the rosin to aid the bow hairs in grabbing the strings by penetrating the scaly surfaces of the hair. The degree of stickiness desired is determined by each player's playing needs and preferences.

The rosin is applied to the taut bow hair in an easy, but firm, motion. It is important to get uniform coverage from frog to point. It is also important to be careful not to break hairs when applying the rosin; care should always be taken to keep the edges of the rosin rounded to protect the hairs. Rosin must be reapplied from time to time, as individual needs dictate.

Never leave your rosin in an overly warm location or in direct sunlight, as it will melt or run, to some degree. Different brands begin to soften at varying temperatures, so let experience be your guide. The rosin will also dry out, in time, so it is best kept in a closed container. Be sure that you play a few notes before you add rosin to your bow. There is no point in adding rosin when you don't need it.

• Mute

Mutes are rubber, plastic, wood, or metal devices that clamp onto the bridge. The mute decreases the output and tone quality of the bass by placing extra mass on the bridge. Naturally, different types and sizes of mutes will have varying effects on any given bass.

Musical compositions will often call for a mute, so it is a good idea to own one. The most standard model fits over your D2 and A2 strings and hangs below the bridge. When needed, you simply reach down and clip it into place.

Heavy mutes, often called "practice mutes" and sometimes made of metal, can be used to practice when volume is a problem. The large amount of mass added to the bridge does alter the feel of an instrument, but if without it one could not practice, the hassle is worth it.

• Stool

Many bassists use stools when performing. There is no advantage or disadvantage to this, only personal preference. A stool is most useful during long rehearsals when the player is sometimes faced with much down time.

It is important not to use the stool as a resting place when performing. Proper body mechanics in the back and arms should always be noted. It is my opinion that stool height should be as close to standing height as possible.

• Wheel

In recent years, it has become commonplace for bassists to use a wheel (or wheels) to facilitate moving their bass from one location to another. Wheels are either fitted into the endpin sleeve or attached to the outside of the case. Either way, the bassist must be careful of the road less traveled. Bumps in the road can lead to cracks in the instrument.

• Musical Terms Dictionary

It is imperative that you procure a dictionary of musical terms. Composers include much information on the page in the form of language, and you may just miss the point if you can't read the instructions.

Italian has been the traditional language for usage in music, but German, French, and English are also commonly used. You may need several dictionaries to cover this subject in its entirety.

Electric

It has already been stated that the electric bass is a crossbreed between the electric guitar and the double bass. However, a detailed look at the physical components of the instrument might lead one to believe that it is most closely related to the electric guitar. Physically, this is true. It can be said that the relationship to the electric guitar is of body, the relationship to the double bass is one of spirit, and the performer adds the mind.

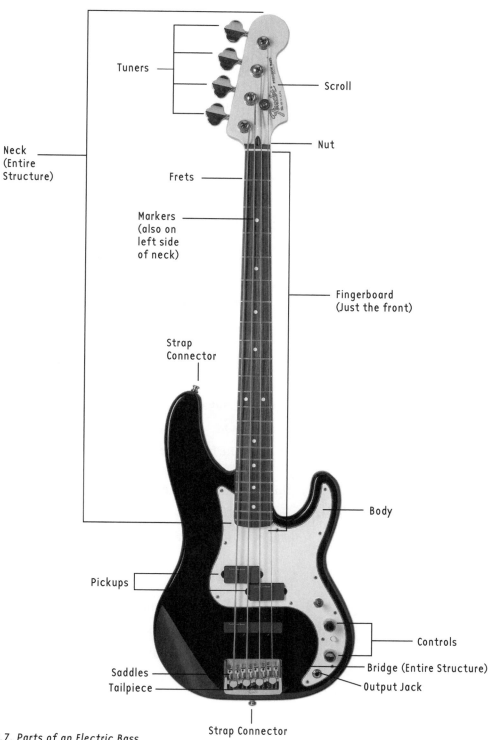

Fig. 2.7. Parts of an Electric Bass

Body

The *body* fastens all of the outlying parts of the instrument together. It is the housing structure for all of the electronics. In addition, it anchors the bridge and attaches to the neck, usually by means of wood screws.

The body is traditionally made of wood, and although almost any hard or decorative wood can be used, maple and ash have been the most popular choices. Most luthiers and the large, mass producing, companies have a "signature" body shape and wood type. The wood of the body can be of one piece, or of two or more glued together. It is also common to laminate different woods together for strength and tone considerations.

Experts disagree on the effect of body materials, size, shape, and weight on the quality of sound produced by an individual instrument, and it is not my place to render this type of judgment here. It is clear, however, that all of these factors do affect the sound of the instrument. Individual performers need to educate themselves as to the variety of woods available and the techniques used to secure these woods together. The body can also be made wholly or in part of a number of other materials. Some of these include graphite, aluminum, and plastic.

There is usually a finish coat on the body. In the case of wood, this can range from a light stain to heavy paint sealed with polyurethane or epoxy. Plastic and graphite are often unfinished, as they can be made to appear finished in the raw state.

Bridge

• Tailpiece

The *tailpiece* sits directly on the bottom of the body and anchors the strings in place. It is usually made of a dense metal but can be made of wood. On some acoustic/electric models, the tailpiece is suspended from the strap connector area, much like the tailpiece of a double bass.

Below the tailpiece, hidden from view within the body, is a ground wire, which connects the electronics to the strings by way of the tailpiece and saddles. This helps to eliminate buzzing and snapping when the player places fingers upon the instrument.

• Saddles

Saddles rest on top of the bridge and are responsible for the delicate settings of string height and length. There is usually one saddle per string, although some instruments have one per two strings, and on others, there is only one saddle mechanism for all four strings.

The saddle is attached to the tailpiece by means of a screw, which in turn governs the length of the string. The saddle also has set screws that rest on the tailpiece, allowing for string height adjustment.

It is also quite common for the saddle tailpiece structure to incorporate a number of locking screws. These screws are usually located to the side of the tailpiece or on the pickup side of the saddle. The purpose of these locking screws is to hold everything in place after adjustments are completed. When making adjustments, care must be taken to loosen these screws first, before any others are loosened, and tighten them last, after all adjustments have been completed.

Additionally, some bridges have set screws designed to raise and lower the entire saddle structure. All of these adjustments allow the player great precision in the setting of the intonation and action.

Pickups

There are numerous pickup types available at present. The most common are magnetic and *electromagnetic* (active). These types of pickups sense the vibration of the metal string just above their position on the body. The position of the pickup, relative to the string, can cause tone and volume differences. A pickup set close to the string will cause a louder, thinner sound. One set farther away will be softer and deeper. Many players believe that setting the pickups close makes for a closer sound, and setting them away creates a more distant sound.

Care should be taken to adjust the pickups so they are not too close to the strings, as the strings can physically damage the pickup upon repeated contact. Too close a setting can also cause signal distortion.

Electromagnetic pickups require outside help to function properly, usually a 9-volt battery or two. This battery powers the signal from the pickup and sends it through a preamp located inside the bass's body.

There are a number of piezo-electric type pickups available today. This is not a magnetic pickup, but rather a pickup that senses the physical vibration of the string movement through a crystal. The crystal senses the movement of the string and reacts by emitting varying amounts of electrical voltage. The voltage is then translated into sound output. These pickups are often called *contact microphones*. The contact microphone can be attached at any location on the instrument where sound is present with varied output results. The most common location for this type of pickup is under the saddles or bridge.

Output and tonal quality vary widely from one pickup to another. The individual player usually doesn't have a choice of pickups unless he has chosen a company that will customize this detail. Most companies install their own pickups or have a limited selection. It is commonplace for players to replace pickups of an older instrument with newer models to update the sound of an instrument. Some players prefer to replace newfangled pickups with older ones to get a vintage sound.

The location of the pickup on the body has a great deal to do with the overall timbre and output of an instrument. This fact has a great deal to do with the location of loops and nodes in the harmonic series of a string, which we will investigate later. Here again, the consumer has little or no control over pickup location on the body, if not customizing. Large companies build their bodies with precut holes for the pickups. In fact, it is the pickup location that often gives an instrument its particular timbre. For example, if you measure from the bridge to each pickup on a Rickenbacker, and compare these measurements to the same made from a Fender Jazz Bass, you will find the distances do not match, and neither does the sound! In general terms, placing the pickup close to the fingerboard will accentuate the lower frequencies, while placing the pickup near the bridge will accentuate the highs.

Pickups also have a variable dimension called *aperture*. The area of aperture is the amount of string that the pickup senses. A small aperture pickup focuses on a small area of string and consequently accentuates the highs; a large aperture pickup will sense more of the lows.

There have been a number of instruments marketed with pickups that were adjustable across the body. The pickup could actually be slid from near the bridge to near the fingerboard. This feature is not common.

Controls

The *controls* are the knobs, dials, and switches located on the body of the instrument. They are usually located on the lower right front, but occasionally, some are placed in other locations.

There are a wide variety of controls, and their manner of functions vary greatly. The most common of these controls include volume, tone, pickup selector, pickup pan, and standby.

One can liken the presence of these controls, and the electronics to follow, to a comparison of cars. One player drives a 1945 Willys Jeep; it goes anywhere, is simple to operate, stands out from the crowd, is simple to fix when broken, has two or three controls, and the player can keep it in excellent repair. Another player likes a 2002 Saab. It's fast, computer driven, looks cool, has all the bells and whistles anyone could wish for, and has too many controls to count—you may need a rental for a week or so when it breaks down!

Electronics

All of the concealed wiring, capacitors, and in some cases computer chips, are called the *electronics* or *guts* of the instrument. Access to the guts is either from under the pick guard or from the back of the body. If an instrument requires a battery, it is usually located near the guts.

Early electric basses were simple beings and had minimal guts. If you open up an early Fender, you will see a capacitor or two, some wires, and the bottoms of the controls. Modern instruments are more complicated. Many instruments have transistor boards inside of them, and some have computer chips.

Most of these guts are best left alone, but some do have adjustable features within that may require the owner's attention. When exploring the inside of a complicated instrument, do some research, contact the company, never rely on guess work, and find a reputable technician who has been recommended to you by other bass players.

Output Jack

The *output jack* is the point at which the electronic signal leaves the instrument en route to the amplifier. Jacks can be monaural or stereo, and a number of styles exist. The jack is usually attached to a metal plate, which is in turn screwed onto the body. The jack attaches to the guts by means of a wire or two. The jack may also protrude a bit from its location on the body.

The jack is a junction area, which is at high risk for wear and accidental damage. The patch cord is plugged in and out of it for every performance. On occasion, the patch cord can get snagged or stepped on causing strain on the jack. The jack can become loose and turn in its socket during normal use. This action can cause the wires on the inside to twist and disconnect. In addition, it can become dirty, rusted, or corroded, especially if the owner lives very near an ocean or in a humid climate. Corrosion, rust, and dirt can cause a foul connection, leading to loss of signal or distortion.

Care should be taken to keep the jack in good, clean working order.

Neck

As with the body, the *neck* is usually made of wood. Maple has been the predominate choice over the years. Recently, however, many manufacturers have begun using a great variety of hard woods for cosmetic and tonal purposes. Construction styles range from one piece to numerous laminations. Of course, other materials, such as graphite and plastic, are also being used.

The necks of most electric basses resemble electric guitar necks more than double-bass necks, but they generally fall in between the two in length. Most manufacturers have distinctive specifications for the design of their necks. The taper, width, and overall shape of a neck are specific to a particular brand and model. It's easy, for example, to spot a Fender copy.

The conventional neck is attached to the body by means of wood screws. These screws may have receivers anchored within the body. The body usually has a carved out area in which to receive the neck snugly. The planes of this junction determine the neck angle. A good fit with the proper angle is critical for stability and sustain. Some instruments have a set-screw adjuster to fine-tune the neck angle. This screw is located under the neck plate, which the screws go through behind the body.

Many instruments feature a neck-through-body construction. The neck actually extends through, and becomes part of the body, leading all the way to the bridge. These necks are usually several, or more, pieces of wood laminated together. This type of construction allows maximum stability and optimum sustain, but does not allow for neck removal.

Most necks have a fingerboard on them. Those that do not have a fingerboard tend to be less stable. A neck without a separate fingerboard has the fingerboard shape fashioned into the actual wood that forms the neck.

Since the electric bass neck is relatively thin, its wood will react noticeably to seasonal changes, especially changes in humidity. The thinner the neck, the greater the reaction. Changes in humidity from season to season can cause wood to swell and shrink. These movements require the performer to make action adjustments on a seasonal basis. Laminated necks, or necks of two or more pieces of wood, are more stable and less apt to bend with the seasons. Thicker necks are also more stable, and the addition of a fingerboard adds lamination and thickness. This is not to say that instruments with thin necks are inferior, only that they bend with the seasons to a greater extent and require more regular adjustments.

The neck is the part of the electric bass most obviously affected by these seasonal changes. Seasonal changes include humidity vs. arid and hot vs. cold. Obviously, extremes are always bad, but I'm sure that most players will keep their basses out of the snow, the desert, the pool, and the sauna! This aside, be careful on a long trip with your bass (in its black gig bag) lying in the back of your hatchback in the sun, or packed in the back of an unheated van in February. Don't set your bass too close to the radiator if you live in New Hampshire; in fact, get a humidifier—a big one! It's good for your health, too.

Rapid changes are the most risky. Rapid movement from a hot club to sub-freezing temperatures out of doors can cause finish cracks. Sun exposure can cause finish cracks and fading.

Excessive moisture may cause wood rot and metal corrosion. These problems can affect all of the parts of your bass.

The normal seasonal changes that affect the neck are easily dealt with when one understands what is happening. As cold weather comes on, we close the windows. As we heat our air, we drive out the humidity. In time, the humidity in the neck of your bass passes to the dry air, causing the wood to shrink. Since your tightened strings are pulling the neck in one direction and the wood has shrunk, the neck gives more in the direction of strain causing your action to rise. The reverse happens in the warmer weather, when you open the windows and turn off the heat. At this time, the wood takes in the humidity and swells, causing your action to go down. This movement will be very regular, as long as you don't move to a new location, so you will be making the same action adjustments each year. Of course, you could move to Hawaii and avoid this problem entirely.

Fingerboard

The *fingerboard* is often called the "fretboard," but sometimes there are no frets present. Stick with "fingerboard."

Fingerboards are fitted to the neck and glued in place. The fit must be perfect to offer optimal stability and sustain. Electric-bass fingerboards usually have a slight side-to-side arch, which fits the contour of the left-hand fingers nicely. This arch need not be as pronounced as that of the double bass, since the instrument is not meant to be bowed, but its presence may be partially attributable to its double-bass genes.

The traditional choice of wood for fingerboards is ebony. Ebony is beautiful, black, very hard, dense, and expensive. It has become more expensive, in recent years, as the supplies dwindle and the demand remains strong. Most ebony is grown in Africa, and the trees mature very slowly.

Rosewood is the next most popular choice of wood, and much of it comes from Brazil. It is a deep reddish brown color and is also quite hard. In the late 1970s, many different varieties of rosewood became popular for cosmetic purposes. Today, of particular note are the many beautiful Oriental rosewoods.

At present, many hard woods are being used for fingerboards, but the standard remains ebony.

Fingerboards are usually not finished, since there are usually frets to protect them from excessive wear. However, if constructed of softer and lighter colored woods, they can be finished to protect them from wear and aid in retention of their original appearance.

The care of a fretless fingerboard is a little more complicated, since when there are no frets present, the wear of the strings is directly on the fingerboard. There are several factors to consider. Round-wound strings cause more abrasion than do flat-wound strings. Harder, denser woods wear away more slowly that do woods that are softer and less dense. Light-colored woods show the stains of everyday playing more than do darker ones.

Usually, when you purchase an instrument constructed with a fingerboard not of ebony or rosewood, it has been finished with an epoxy or urethane product, so you will not need to make the decision of whether to finish or not. If you are customizing or buying a well-used instrument, you may be faced with this decision.

Here are some points to remember. All wood wears down in time, but as is the case with ebony, it might take fifty years or so. Softer woods wear faster, and ruts in the fingerboard can ruin your sound. These ruts can be sanded out with care and guidance from someone experienced in the procedure. Round-wound strings rut a fingerboard faster than flat-wound strings do. Finish products will also wear down in time. Adding a finish to the fingerboard will change the timbre of your bass, so if you like the sound you get with no finish, it may be worth it to learn how to care for your fingerboard as it wears.

The fingerboard is the central point at which we touch our instrument. It is a connecting point that can become a personal friend for life. Special care needs to be given to such a fine friend.

Frets

Frets allow for easy, accurate intonation and are generally made of a nickel/copper/zinc alloy. Fret wire comes in a variety of gauges, and much care must be taken to install it properly. The wire must be clipped from the spool, accurately inserted into the precut slot, seated properly, and finished, or dressed, so as to have no rough edges. A skilled craftsman will have the ability to calibrate the proper height requirements of each fret, or this task may be accomplished by a machine. I prefer the former.

Bassists who play a great deal in just a few positions sometimes wear out three or four frets but not the others. As this happens, the instrument will begin to buzz in the affected area. To correct this problem, the unaffected frets can be ground down to match the worn frets, or in time, all of the frets will need to be replaced. This is not a job for the novice, and it is an excellent time for a trip to your favorite technician.

Nut

The *nut* is the point at which the speaking length of the strings ends on the neck. The strings are often clamped behind the nut by use of an eyelet or small horizontal clamp to ensure good contact. Many instruments have slanted scrolls to ensure good contact. The nut has slots filed into it in which the strings rest. If good contact is not made at this point, undesirable buzzing and poor sustain may result. In addition, the slots, or grooves, must not be so deep as to swallow the string nor so shallow as to let the string slip to the side.

The overall height of the nut is also of significant importance. A nut set too high makes playing in the lower positions quite painful, as the strings will be well above the fingerboard. A nut set too low does not allow the notes to sound fully. Very few instruments have adjustable nuts, but this is not of great concern; once a nut is set up, it should be positioned permanently. The standard height of the nut allows for a business card to pass between the G string and the first fret.

The nut can be made of plastic, bone, metal, or wood, and this material will affect the open-string timbre of the instrument. By altering the material, it is possible to "cover up" the open strings. Occasionally, the nut can simply be a fret with a clamping mechanism behind it.

Scroll

The *scroll*, sometimes called the "scroll box," "head stalk," or "head piece," is located at the outer end of the neck. It anchors the tuners, and each company tends to have its own characteristic shape. There are instruments with no scroll, notably the Steinberger, which allow for tuning in the bridge area. The instrument manufacturer's logo is often placed on the scroll.

Tuners

The *tuners* are attached to the scroll by a nut or small screws. Tuners are also referred to as *machines*, and some "older" players still call them *pegs*. In truth, electric basses were never built with true pegs. A tuner is made up of a shaft attached to a gear wheel and tuning key, which fits into the teeth of the gear wheel. Oftentimes, this mechanism is enclosed, but the Fender style is exposed and easy to understand. As the tuning key is turned, it moves the wheel. This turns the shaft upon which the string is wound, thus tightening or loosening the string. The presence of several right angles does not allow the string to loosen by itself; consequently, the string remains tuned.

Truss Rod

A great many instruments have a *truss rod* buried within the fingerboard length of their necks. This rod is placed to allow for manipulation of the neck bow. The bow of the neck is its curvature. An amount of bow is necessary to allow the strings to vibrate without slashing the frets or fingerboard. The bow can be affected by weather, string gauge, and age.

The truss rod is securely fitted into the neck, usually just beneath the fingerboard, and a screwing type mechanism is attached to one end to allow for adjustments. Sometimes, this adjustment point is at the neck body joint, and sometimes, it is at the base of the scroll. In either case, as the screw is tightened, the neck bow is adjusted. Some necks have metal stabilizer bars that work with the truss rod to guarantee that the neck shape will remain uniform at all times. There are a number of instruments that have multiple truss rods to aid stability and bow adjustment.

As a string vibrates, it takes up a certain amount of space—the longer the string, the more the space. If the fingerboard or frets are in this space, the string will hit them as it vibrates. The correct bowing of the neck allows for the string to clear these objects. This bow must not be too much, due to the fact that as it increases, the closing of notes by the left hand becomes difficult, and fretted intonation becomes noticeably incorrect.

The truss rod works in conjunction with the saddles to fine-tune the action.

Markers

Markers are often placed on the front and player's side of the fingerboard. These markers are intended to help players find their way quickly and accurately around the instrument. Many instruments have abandoned the front markers for lavish designs. Markers and designs are called *inlay* in that they are laid into the neck after construction as a finishing touch. Materials used for the inlay include ivory, mother of pearl, bone, brass, silver, and gold, to mention a few. One can create an inlay in wood using other woods also.

An inlay can be a delicate location on your instrument, so treat these areas with care. Inlay on the front of a fretless fingerboard can be a special problem, since the inlay will feel the full impact of performance. It would also be next to impossible to sand or plane a fretless neck with inlays.

The location and placement of side markers is standard, and as with many other features, you have no choice about this arrangement unless you customize. It appears that the presence and location of these markers originated from the electric guitar.

Strap and Strap Connections

Most players use a *strap* when performing. Your strap should be comfortable, and it must fit your back. Wide is better than narrow, and soft is better than stiff. The length of the strap is important, as it sets up the performance angles of both your hands.

Every person is shaped differently, and it is difficult to dictate performance stance in a book such as this, but several rules of thumb may be helpful.

Circles are always better than sharp angles. If you stand with your bass strapped over your back and hanging around diaphragm height, you will notice several things. If you place your left hand in proper playing position, you should be able to draw a circle from your shoulder, through your elbow, through your hand and out your fingertips, and back to your shoulder. Now, place your right hand in playing position. Can you see the circle? Granted, these are not perfect circles, but maybe your strap needs a slight adjustment to come closer to a circle for your body size. You may never get the circles perfectly round, but remember, nobody is perfect. You may also find the need to sacrifice one circle to improve the other. A good teacher can be of great service in an area such as this.

On the body of the bass, you will have some strap connections. The location of these connections determines the natural balance of your instrument. Some connectors are not movable, but most can be moved. By moving these connectors small distances, the hanging shape of your instrument can be changed dramatically.

These are not things that *need* to be changed but things that *can* be changed. Think about your back, your arm and hand angles, and your fingers, and the circles I spoke of. Take a look in the mirror, if you are considering adjusting the strap length or moving the strap connectors. If your bass is too high on your body, your right wrist and elbow will form sharp angles. If your bass is too low on your body, your left wrist will form a sharp angle. A compromise position works best for most players. Oftentimes, the right adjustment is a combination of adjusting the strap length and moving one or both of the strap connectors. My best advice is to consult with a stance-healthy professional who has been playing for fifteen or more years. Someone such as this will have a great deal of wisdom to pass along to the novice in regards to performance posture.

Strings

The variety of strings available today is nearly endless. There are a number of factors to consider when purchasing strings.

It is imperative that you match the length of string to the scale of your bass. You can discover the scale of your bass by measuring the G string from the nut to the saddle. Most electric basses are long scale, which means that this vibrating length of the string is 34 inches. An extra-long scale of 36 inches and a medium scale of 32 inches are also common. Short-scale strings for shorter instruments are available. Experimentation with different scale sets may be necessary for the numerous instruments that do not match these standards. The common-sized Modulus is a 35-inch scale, and in some cases, a long-scale string will fit this bass. In all cases, you want the silk thread wrapping, if any is present, to be behind the nut when the string is tuned up.

Some strings are said to be *open* or *exposed* core. This means that there is little or no winding at the point where the string rests on the saddle. The winding is usually removed or tapered from the lower, fatter strings to reduce friction at the saddle, thus increasing sustain. Specific saddle adjustments will be needed to bring these strings to the proper height, due to the lack of wrapping at the saddle.

The string itself is a steel wire wrapped with various layers of thinner wire to achieve the desired thickness or *gauge*. The outer wire is made of different alloys, some of which are harder than others, accounting for much of the tonal differences from brand to brand.

The actual surface that the performer touches is said to be *flat* or *round*. Round-wound strings can be half round, quarter round, ground round, and the like, denoting that the edge has been filed to some degree. A flat-wound string gives a deep thumpy sound made popular by players like James Jamerson. A fully round-wound string can achieve a brilliant tone similar to Chris Squire's.

For many years, the standard was the Rotosound medium-gauge jazz bass set. If you are searching for the right string sound, this is still a good place to start. If you like the Motown sound, try Fender flats.

The *gauge* of a string relates to the eventual tightness of the string when it is tuned up. A 40 gauge G string will be looser than a 45, since it will take more tension to tune the 45 up to pitch. All other things being equal, the 45 will have a deeper tone than the 40.

If you are looking for odd gauges, they can be found, since there are a number of companies that custom wind strings to any requested gauge. Of course, you will pay for this service.

String shopping can be an expensive venture. Try swapping sets with your friends to see how a string will feel. If your strings seem to have lost their sound, try cleaning them with isopropyl alcohol. This can bring them back to life for a time. Be careful to keep the alcohol away from the finish of your bass, as it may affect the luster.

Look for a string that feels and sounds right. This is a relative judgment, since we all stroke the string with our own personal touch, and we each hear as individuals, so experimentation is always necessary. The touch on the instrument is the key to many of the great player's styles, so some added attention spent finding the right strings is not wasted.

Accessories

• Amplifier

It is not the scope of this text to explore the subject of amplifiers in depth, but a few words are in order.

Your electric bass is useless without an amplifier, leading me to believe that the beauty of a fine instrument goes wasted without proper amplification. We relate more closely to our instrument than we do to our amplifier, due, I think, to the fact that we hold our instruments in our arms and manipulate them with our hands and fingers. The same cannot be said about an amplifier, except during setup and tear down. But your amplifier will make or break your sound, and in many cases, will be a greater financial investment than your bass.

So, which comes first, the chicken or the egg? In this case, I believe that the bass comes first. The amplifier compliments and brings out the best of the bass. The amplifier is chosen for its specific attributes, which lend themselves to your instrument's strengths and your amplification needs. The amplifier may also be able to support some of the inherent weaknesses of a given bass, covering dead spots or filling in lost frequencies.

Some amplifiers have characteristic sounds and are often chosen for this reason. Most players, however, expect their amplifier to reproduce the sound that they believe is inside of their bass.

• D Tuner

The *D tuner* is a modified tuning machine that allows a string to be lowered in pitch at the flip of a lever. Although it can replace any tuner, it is usually used on the E string to extend the range of the string lower. The original intention was to lower the pitch to D1, hence the name "D" tuner. This device is also called a Hipshot, after a company that makes excellent quality versions of them.

D tuners come in many styles, intended to replace the original E-string machine on most instruments. If you can find a replacement intended for your instrument, you need only unscrew and remove the original tuner and replace it with the new D tuner. It should fit right in, and even the attachment screw holes should line up. If you need to reshape the hole in the scroll that the tuner fits into, you should find a technician to accomplish the task.

It is possible for this device to extend the range of the E string lower than D1, or one whole step, but in so doing, care must be taken to be sure that in lessening the tension of the E string the remaining strings don't veer sharp. When D tuning very low, the E string becomes very flabby, and timbre and pitch can leave much to be desired.

• Patch Cord

It is an electric bass, and yes, it is useless without a patch cord. It has always amazed me to see a bassist come to a lesson, or an ensemble, or a gig, without a patch cord. "I forgot my patch cord, man. Can you lend me one?" Would you like me to play the part for you too?

My suggestion is that you need to purchase not one, not two, but at least three quality patch cords of the length required by your present performing situations. Buy some quality gear. It won't hurt. Today's coaxial cables offer excellent shielding and clear conductance. In 1971, I purchased two Whirlwind Cobra cords. Whirlwind stopped making the Cobra in 1985. When I bought mine, it came with a lifetime guarantee. I did send one back once, after one of my buddies pulled it out of my bass with his foot! It was promptly repaired and returned.

These chords were very expensive at the time, maybe $15 to $20 each. I still own them. In fact, I use one for all my gigs and the other is an extra, rarely used. I have other cords that I carry to gigs also, just in case. Usually, I end up lending one of them to a guitar player. Good equipment, well cared for, can last a lifetime.

By the way, if your amplifier needs to be attached to its speakers by an outside wire, a regular patch cord is not the right cord to use. It is best to use heavy-gauge speaker wire. Use the shortest length possible, so your signal isn't wasted in the transfer.

• Pick

When the electric bass was young, in the 1950s and 1960s, many players plucked the strings with a pick. This influence was handed down by the guitar side of the family. In time, use of the pick became less prevalent, but today, many players still prefer the feel and sound of a pick.

Electric bass picks are somewhat larger than standard guitar picks, and they come in a number of shapes. The stiffness of the pick is controlled by the material of which it is made and the thickness of this material. A thick, pointed pick produces a strong percussive sound, whereas a soft, rounded pick produces a much more mellow sound.

Picks are usually made of plastic or felt.

- **Mute**

Many older electric basses were equipped with a mute. The mute was a sort of thin foam strip glued inside of the bell. The bell was a decorative piece that covered the bridge. If the bell was attached to the instrument, the foam strip would press slightly against the vibrating strings, thus acting as a mute. The effect of this mute was more like that of a muffler, as it deadened the string sound and sustain substantially. This type of mute could easily be removed from the bell permanently, but most players preferred to completely remove the bell as it interfered with easy action adjustments. Modern instruments do not have a bell or the attached mute. At present, there is no standard mechanical mute for the electric bass.

It is possible to mute using the right hand. Right-hand muting is generally accomplished by use of a non-plucking finger lightly dampening the plucked string or allowing the heel of the thumb or hand to rest lightly on the plucked string near the bridge causing the muted sound. Muting with the left hand can be accomplished by placing the fingers just above the frets so as to allow the flesh to dampen the vibrating string. On a fretless, applying more soft flesh to the string causes a muted effect.

- **Pedals**

You may want to add a pedal or two to your rig. This is not a necessity. Pedals add more equipment in need of upkeep. Pedals need to be kept clean and batteries will need to be changed, often. You will need more working patch cords and possibly a snake.

Did I mention that you will need a bag to carry all of this gear in? Don't forget that you will never be able to load all of this stuff into a car. It's time for a hatchback, wagon, or van.

- **Musical Terms Dictionary**

Please refer to the dictionary section under "double," earlier in this chapter.

CHAPTER 3
Repairs, Adjustments, and Maintenance

Major structural repairs and intricate adjustments to double or electric basses are best left to a qualified technician. Repairs related to pickups, controls, and other internal electronics are beyond the grasp of the average owner and should be avoided. It is imperative that you know and trust someone who has attained all of the knowledge necessary to care for your bass when major ailments occur or when in-depth work in needed.

Seldom will you find a technician who works on both double and electric basses, so those players who double will be looking for two technicians. Double-bass players will need a bow rehairer, too.

There are, however, a number of simple adjustments and minor repairs that you can do easily. With a little practice, taking the care that your instrument deserves, you will be able to perform many of these tasks needed to keep your bass in tip-top shape.

Double

Changing Strings

It is an easy, although time consuming, task to change the strings. The instrument should be placed on its back. If you are not prepared to reset the soundpost, you must be careful that it remain erect throughout the string-changing process. Do not take all of the pressure off of the bridge unless you intend to remove the bridge temporarily. Rest the bass on a rug or blanket so that the back does not become scratched.

Observe the manner and direction in which the strings are wound inside of the pegbox. The strings should not crowd each other and should be wound in an orderly fashion, so as to allow easy tightening and loosening without interfering with each other's movement. Change the strings one at a time by loosening each machine and slipping the ball end of the string out of its fitting in the tailpiece, doing the reverse to replace the new string. Allow a couple inches of string to protrude through the insertion hole in the machine shaft or peg to ensure that the string will hold as it is initially wound.

If the bridge is located properly, ensure that it does not move. The bridge has a tendency to lean towards the fingerboard, due to the pressure exerted by the strings over time. It is especially apt to lean this way when changing strings, causing an accidental fall to be a strong possibility. Be certain that the bridge remains up straight throughout this process, checking it often. Applying a little pencil lead in the bridge's string grooves will facilitate the movement of the strings as they are tightened, thus taking some stress off of the bridge.

Save your old strings for emergencies or charity to needy bassists.

Gluing Seams

Basses often develop cracks. Any crack within a piece of wood is best repaired by a professional, but many cracks in seams can be repaired by the owner. You will need some fine-grit sandpaper, hide glue, clamps, some small scraping tools, and plenty of patience.

Cracks commonly develop between the front and sides or the back and sides. These cracks can be caused by seasonal stress or physical abuse. In either case, if the crack is located along a glue joint, repair is simple.

The glue used to hold the seams together is usually a water-based glue. I use hide glue. It can be purchased in liquid or crystal forms and comes with application instructions. When in place, if heated, wetted, or stressed, the glue will let go. Under stressful conditions, this allows the seams to open, rather than the wood to split. A true crack in the wood is much more serious than a simple seam fracture.

All of the old glue must be cleaned out of the crack. You will need lots of thin sandpaper, maybe an emery board, and some very small scraping tools. I procured some old dental tools from my dentist that work just fine for this job. If there is a great deal of old glue, a thin knife, heated, will help to melt it away. Just slip it into the seam, and wipe the area with a warm, wet rag.

When the area is cleaned up, you are ready to glue and clamp. You must have all of your materials ready, as these next steps proceed quickly.

The clamps must be large enough to accommodate the depth of the instrument from front to back. There are clamps made for this job, but you can easily fashion them from small

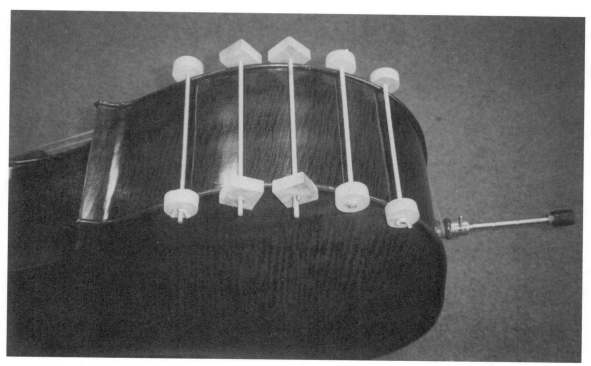

Fig. 3.1. Double Bass Clamps

wooden squares and miniature axles of the right length. You now only need nuts to hold everything together. I have a friend who, in an emergency, fashioned wonderful clamps from thread spools. He still uses them today.

You will need plenty of clamps. I like to use as many as I can to ensure that the surfaces are in total contact. For a 6-inch crack, I would use at least four clamps, so you can see that with larger cracks you will need many clamps. Gather up at least ten or twelve clamps.

The hide glue must be mixed, if necessary, and is usually applied hot. Be sure to coat all exposed surfaces, but do not be overly generous. Clamp the entire area being worked on, and carefully wipe away any glue that has squeezed through the joint. Do not clamp so tightly as to distort the wood, but ensure good contact all along the seam. Set the bass aside for about a day to heal. Clean the glue off your tools. After the setting period, unclamp the seam, and be sure the clamps are clean, ready for your next repair.

Do not be tempted to use wood glue. Wood glue will not give way, if stressed, and it will cause the seam to be stronger than the wood itself. Under these conditions, the wood will crack, rather than the seam letting go. Wood glue is also extremely difficult to remove when repair is necessary. Consult a technician if you need help.

Care of the Body

The body of your bass should be treated like a fine wood antique. In many cases, that is exactly what it is. Be sure you have a padded, insulating case that offers protection during travel. Always move slowly when carrying your bass through crowded areas, especially if it is out of the case.

The finish on instruments ranges from heavy varnish to a light stain. This makes it difficult to recommend proper treatment. Determine the type of finish that has been applied to your bass, and procure the product necessary to aid in the protection of the instrument's wood. In most cases, an oil-based furniture polish intended for use on quality furniture will suffice. I prefer a light lemon-oil-based product. Regular applications will protect the wood and keep the instrument clean.

Cleaning Strings and Fingerboard

The strings and the fingerboard become excessively soiled with oils from the hands and rosin. It is important to clean these items, as the buildup of soil affects the sound of the instrument adversely.

Isopropyl alcohol of 91% solution can be used for this purpose. Place the alcohol on a rag and rub the individual string up and down, being sure to clean it entirely. Spend extra time in the area of bowing. Then reapply the alcohol to a clean portion of the rag and clean the fingerboard. Be very careful not to drip the alcohol onto the body of the instrument, as it may cause a stain. Be sure to wipe off all of the alcohol.

If you would like to treat the fingerboard, many people use a very light lemon oil for this purpose. However, most players do not treat the fingerboard, but rather allow the natural oils produced by the hand to accomplish this task.

Exposed gut strings require special treatment. Any frays in the gut must be carefully cut away, and the string can be cleaned with a mild soap and water solution. The clean string can then be treated with lemon oil, or the like, to help prolong its life.

Soundpost Adjustment

To adjust the soundpost, you need the proper tool. If you own a bass that requires frequent adjustments, or have an instrument fitted with several posts to accommodate seasonal changes, it might be worth your while to purchase a soundpost tool. A small light and a dental style mirror are also very helpful when moving or adjusting the soundpost.

Finely adjusting the location of the soundpost causes output changes in the bass. The luthier has determined the proper location of the post, but owners often find a need to adjust this

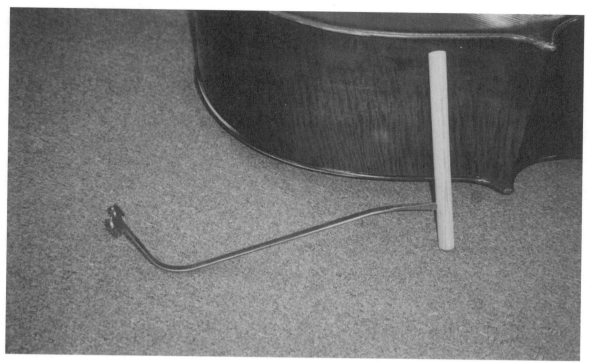

Fig. 3.2. Soundpost Tool and Soundpost

location. You first need to determine the soundpost location desired either through experience or trial and error. Loosen, but do not remove, the strings. Keep enough tension on the bridge to hold it firmly in place. Using the tool, move the post as necessary. When in place, it should run straight from the front to the back, being about a thumb's thickness below the right foot of the bridge, and coming in complete flush contact on both the front and back.

Many bassists own this tool so that they can set the post back up in the case of an accidental fall. After the emergency has passed, they take the bass to their technician for proper precise placement.

Adjusting the Action

If your bridge has adjustors on it, you will be able to adjust the height of the strings. Seasonal changes affect the double bass as its wood content reacts to changes in humidity. In dryer weather the action lowers, and in more humid seasons the action raises.

In adjusting your bridge, the adjustors should never be extended beyond about an inch. This much extension indicates that your bridge is cut too low, and as the extension reaches this level, the bridge begins to weaken. In adjusting height, the adjustors should also be moved in tandem as much as possible. If one side of your bridge needs to be raised well above the other, this is an indication of a misshaped bridge. A shape such as this can cause the bridge to pull to one side.

When initially adding the adjustors to a bridge, it is best to start with a bridge that fits perfectly during the humid season. Have the technician place the adjustors, removing only enough wood to accommodate the wheels. You should be able to set the adjustors all the way down during humid times and raise as needed in dry seasons.

Compensating for the Lack of Humidity

The greatest enemy of the double bass is dry weather. Dryness causes wood to crack. If at all possible, try to avoid dry conditions for any extended period of time. If this is not possible, added humidity via a humidifier is helpful. Many players use *dampits* placed in the *f* holes. A dampit is a spongelike wick placed inside of a long rubber tube that has holes in it. The dampit is soaked in water to fill the wicks and hung inside of the bass via the *f* holes. Do not allow the dampits to drip water into the bass, as this can cause rotting. Also, be aware that dampits add but a small amount of water to the air and offer only a slight solution. A technician once told me that using a dampit was like trying to heat a room with a match. A large humidifying system will be best for the health of your bass, and it can do a great deal for your own health as well. When using a large humidifying system, be careful not to add too much humidity in very cold weather, as this will cause condensation to form on the inside surfaces of your dwelling. This may lead to rot around your windows or within your walls, a more expensive problem to remedy than a crack in your bass.

You can use a hygrometer to measure the room's humidity. They are not expensive, give accurate humidity readings, and can save much on repair bills.

Bassists often find that their instruments self adjust from day to day, and from location to location. This is caused by mini differences in the climate of different locations in close proximity to one another. You may need to allow a bit of time for your bass to adjust to the climate at any given gig. This is a perfect excuse to show up early, thus allowing your bass to acclimate itself to its surroundings before you need to perform. The leader of the gig will also appreciate your punctuality.

Electric

Changing Strings

The great majority of strings hold into the bridge hole by means of a ball end; they are inserted through the machine shaft for tightening.

Remove all of the strings from the instrument by unwinding the machines. When the strings are off, take advantage of the open fingerboard and do some house cleaning. This is a great time to conduct a general cleanup of the entire instrument.

The new string must be inserted through the bridge hole and run up the neck to the appropriate machine. The machine shaft has a slit running across it and a hole within this slit. The string is inserted into the hole, bent at a 90-degree angle, and brought through the slit. The string can then be wound from top to bottom of the shaft until tuned. Occasionally, individual strings must be cut shorter to fit properly onto the shaft. String-changing experience with your bass and chosen brand of strings will lead you to make the proper cut before tuning.

As you tune a string, it often becomes twisted. You cannot see this twist but you can relieve it. As the string becomes almost taut, relieve the twist by pulling the ball end away from the bridge hole. This action will remove unneeded stress to the inner core of the string when it is tuned to pitch.

Save used strings, especially G and D strings, as replacements or for emergency string-break repairs.

Care of the Body and Neck

Most electric bodies have a hard, lacquer type finish. The back of the neck is also usually finished in this fashion. The biggest danger to this type of finish is chipping. Always exercise care not to bump the finished wood with hard, pointed objects. Extreme cold and heat can also crack the finish and should be avoided. A good finish can be cleaned with a mild soap-and-water solution, but be very careful not to drip water onto or into the instrument. It is electric.

The fact that your instrument is finished does not exempt it from seasonal changes, if it is of wood construction. Unless all of the wood is completely sealed, moisture will find its way in and out as necessary through the unfinished spaces provided. Look closely. You will find unfinished spots around the truss rod, in the body cutouts, where the neck fits the body, at the fingerboard, and inside all of the screw holes. Don't forget all of those little cracks and chips you caused. Humidity will flow in and out of these openings as the seasons change, causing the expansion and contraction that we all must deal with. If your instrument does not have a finish, then you should treat it like the body of a double bass.

A certain amount of normal wear and tear occurs to instruments that are well used. The wear spots on an instrument can reveal a great deal about the player. In time, the owner's fingers will fit into some of these wear spots, which are commonly located around the pickup and on the back of the neck. Most players like this wearing, as it lends a personal feel to the instrument.

Cleaning Strings and Fingerboard

Electric bass strings can be cleaned in a similar fashion to double-bass strings. Round-wound strings require more attention to the cleaning process, as oily dirt can hide in the windings very easily. A side-to-side rotating motion with the rag, while rubbing the length of the string, will usually free this dirt.

An unfinished rosewood or ebony fingerboard can be cleaned as you would a double-bass fingerboard. If the fingerboard is finished, cleaning can be done as for the other finished parts.

Frets can become corroded through heavy use or abuse. Corrosion, and other dirt in the fret area, can be removed by cleaning with a toothbrush or the careful use of a small scraping tool.

Adjusting the Truss Rod

Your instrument should have a truss rod tool included with it. If you don't have this tool, I suggest that you find one. Contact your manufacturer, or take your bass to a hardware store, and purchase the appropriate tool. The truss rod tool is usually similar to a hexagonal wrench. This type of wrench is often called an "Allen wrench," and in fact, most truss rod tools are Allen wrenches. Hexagonal fittings can be male or female, and unfortunately, so can the truss rod fitting. It is also unfortunate that the size of the fitting also varies from instrument to instrument. It is for this reason that I reiterate, the tool should be included with the instrument.

Carefully consider your reasons for adjusting the truss rod before doing so. Most truss rods can be adjusted with the instrument strung up, but you may need to lower the string tension to facilitate the movement of a tight or frozen rod. If the rod seems jammed or very tight, it is best to take the instrument to a technician for service. The fitting of the rod can become stripped through repeated use or by using a wrench that is not quite the right size. This is a major problem. If the rod becomes stripped, it can no longer be moved in the intended manner. This requires a trip to the technician for surgery.

As stated earlier, the truss rod adjusts the bow of the neck. In no case should this bow be so great as to make playing difficult or cause intonation discrepancies. The adjustment of the rod should be slight; if major adjustment is needed, action adjustments are incorrect.

If your instrument is set up properly, you may never need to adjust this rod. The most common adjustments are made to accommodate seasonal changes.

As the weather dries, the moisture exits the neck, causing it to contract. This contraction allows the scroll to pull forward from the tension of the strings, thus raising the action. The proper adjustment to the rod will push the neck back into the proper position.

As the seasons change again, the air becomes generally more humid. The moisture flows back into the neck, causing it to expand. This action works against the action of the strings, and the action lowers. The owner now must adjust the truss rod back to the original position.

It is common for these adjustments to be identical from year to year.

Many instruments are very sensitive to changes in the weather and require more frequent adjustments. Many players require their instruments to be in perfect setup at all times, making regular truss rod adjustments more commonplace. A fine-quality instrument will have a truss rod that is easily accessible and easily manipulated, making this adjustment convenient for even the novice, but care must always be taken to not overadjust. Always be sure that you know why you are adjusting your instrument, or consult a qualified technician for assistance.

Setting the Action

The *action* is defined as the general height of the strings manipulated by the saddles. It is important to note that the string length is also manipulated at the saddles, but this adjustment has little to do with the action. Manipulation of string length is an adjustment intended to set the intonation.

The most common action adjustment is accomplished by means of two screws that go directly through each saddle and give it relative height under the pressure of the taut string. By raising or lowering these screws, one can manipulate the string height in the bridge area.

This adjustment also governs the playability of the instrument in the upper and middle register, as long as the truss rod is adjusted correctly. You may recall that the nut sets the height of the strings in the lower register. Always adjust the truss rod and nut (if it's adjustable) first, saving the action setting for last.

Later in this book, I will discuss setting the intonation. Nut, truss rod, and action adjustments must be done prior to setting the intonation. After setting the intonation initially, one may need to repeat some steps, but this is rarely the case, as the instrument would have been unplayable to be so out of alignment.

The action is often set to an arch matching the arch of the fingerboard. This ensures that the distances from fret to string are the same throughout the instrument, from string to string. Small compensations may need to be made for the thicker strings.

Once your action is set, you will usually be able to make any seasonal adjustments necessary from the truss rod.

Many instruments have set screws, in various locations on the bridge, not related to setting the action. These are lock screws, which lock all of the movable parts in place once the setting of the action is complete. Study your instrument carefully before you start turning screws.

So, how do you determine where to set your action? Experimentation is your only solution. The action should never be set so low as to allow for string buzzing under normal playing conditions. Low action generally gives a more metallic sound. Raising the action yields a more rounded sound and allows more intense playing, physically.

Action that is set low allows for less effort of the left hand, and many players believe that a low action setting increases the ability to play fast. But many players with high action have no problem playing fast, disproving this misconception. If your action is set high, you need to expend more effort to play, so you require more physical chops. This may require more practice time to keep your muscles and calluses at peak form. Good physical facility is achievable on the instrument with almost any action setting that allows the player to produce good sound. Experimentation is recommended.

Stripped Screw Holes

During the lifetime of an instrument, there are many occasions when screws need to be loosened and tightened. Strap connector screws become loose through normal use. Neck screws must be removed to perform work on a detachable neck. Pick-guard screws must be removed to access the guts of a Fender. Since these screws grip into wood, it is only natural that the holes may become stripped, on occasion.

A stripped screw hole can be repaired by either jamming it full of small slivers of wood and wood glue, or by filling the hole with a mixture of wood glue and saw dust. In either case, the surface of the hole must be brought level with the surrounding area and the mixture should be allowed to dry for a day or so. Once dried, the screw can be replaced into the same location. For larger screws, a pilot hole may need to be drilled. Be sure this hole is of a smaller diameter than the screw.

Replacing Screwed-On Parts

There are a number of parts that are merely screwed into place. Strap connectors, machines, and pick guards are the most common of these. It has always seemed silly to me to pay someone else to tighten a few screws. If you can remove a part, it is just a matter of reversing your actions to replace it.

Always be careful not to over tighten. This is especially true in the case of small brass set screws often found behind fine tuners. Overtightening causes the head of the screw to pop off, leaving the screw in the hole with no way to get it out.

CHAPTER 4

Fingerboard Theory

This discussion of fingerboard theory has two components. Think of these components as physical and spiritual, as tangible and intangible, or as animate and inanimate. However you view them, you cannot avoid their far-reaching implications to all bass players.

We choose our fingerings based upon our past experiences. They are closely related and very much dependent upon each other.

On the spiritual side, there is our system of tuning. A tuning system is a group of notes organized around each other by geometric means. There have been many tuning systems used throughout musical history. These systems range from just a few notes to much larger scales incorporating varying numbers of notes, sometimes far greater than the twelve used most commonly today.

The ratios used in a tuning system are created by placing the cps (cycles per second) of one note over the cps of another. For example, the pitches 100 cps and 200 cps are in the ratio 1/2, or one octave. The frequencies of 100 cps and 400 cps create the ratio 1/4, or two octaves.

Other ratios yield other intervals. Since there are an endless number of fractions, it follows that there are an endless number of intervals available. Different tuning systems are characterized by the ratios that they include. These ratios are organized so that performers can understand what they are hearing and perform with their fellow musicians.

As performers, we don't need to know all of the theory behind building scales using fractions. We are concerned with sound relationships. Our primary concern is to aurally understand our present tuning system.

The tuning system in use at any given time demands that only notes within that system be used. Music has evolved throughout all of mankind's history, and our present system of relating to each other tonally is a product of all of this evolution. If one veers out of this system, one is said to be "out of tune," and there is nothing worse than an out-of-tune bass player. We are prisoners, bound within the system, and most of us don't even realize it.

But being in a prison such as this is not so terrible. You still have many wonderful colors to hear and create. There are at least twelve major keys, and many more, if you posses the depth of knowledge to consider them. It is a challenge that most of us welcome, to play in tune, and we respect anyone who can consistently do it well. Besides, being out of tune is such a relative point that I challenge you to find two musicians who can agree on its exact definition. Brilliant people have been notating music for centuries, and much of this material is as exciting today as it was when it was conceived. Most of us have the utmost respect for those among us who can read with emotion and sound so natural, every time they perform.

And then, on our physical side, there is the physical arrangement of the notes on the instrument. This arrangement is also predetermined for us and has everything to do with how we think and how we react musically. Those of us who double on electric and double basses appreciate this similarity between the two instruments, but few realize the far-reaching implications caused by this arrangement. There is also a physical arrangement within our hands that comes into play. Would the bass be fashioned as it is today if we had six fingers on each hand?

Equal Temperament

As modern-day musicians—at least, in most of the Western world—we relate to a system of tuning with twelve equal chromatic steps per octave. We call this *equal temperament*. It is important to understand what equal temperament means and why we use it, as it is at the very foundation of the music we perceive and perform every day.

To begin with, the tuning system we use is more correctly called the *twelve-step equal-tempered* system. The reality is that any number of equal steps can be placed within an octave and we are currently using twelve. The octave is the only unmovable interval, since it is a repetition of itself and therefore must be kept in any logical tuning system. I do not believe that humankind is ready for music that lacks repeated intervals at the octave. It is the twelve-step equal-tempered system that most closely matches the tuning systems used initially by the ancient Greeks, moving forward in time to the age of Bach, and beyond. Consequently, in most of the Western world, it has become the standard tuning system in use today.

Many years ago, a fellow named Pythagoras was sitting around thinking. While thinking, he heard some local blacksmiths pounding on spear tips with iron hammers. He noticed that the hammers gave out a distinctive ping as they struck the anvil below the spear tip. He also noticed that the hammers didn't all sound the same. In fact, he found that heavier hammers sounded lower than lighter ones. Intrigued by his observations, he listened more closely, and he noticed that as the hammers of different pitches struck together, forming intervals, some of them sounded nice and some did not. He was observing what we now call *consonance* and *dissonance*.

Now, since Pythagoras was a mathematician, he began to study what he was hearing, in an attempt to understand it in numerical terms. He realized that the intervals that were most pleasing to his ear, the consonant ones, were produced by hammers whose weights, expressed as fractions, related to each other in one of three ways: 1/2, 2/3, or 3/4. He theorized that all musical intervals could be somehow built from these three fractions. His study eventually led him to build the first major scale by using just these three fractions, which he called *super particular ratios*. In later times, in attempts to improve his scale, these three ratios were expanded by other theorists to be any ratio N + 1/N, or 5/4, 6/5, 7/6, and so on.

Pythagoras now applied his theory to strings and came up with the following, where string length = L:

$$L \times 1/2 = \text{up 1 octave}$$

$$L \times 2/3 = \text{up a perfect 5th}$$

$$L \times 3/4 = \text{up a perfect 4th}$$

The inverses were also true:

$$L \times 2/1 = \text{down an octave}$$

$$L \times 3/2 = \text{down a perfect 5th}$$

$$L \times 4/3 = \text{down a perfect 4th}$$

Now all he needed was to fill in the cracks. By using just these ratios, inverses included, he made the first major scale as applied to a string:

$$\text{Do–Do}' = \text{Do} \times 1/2$$

$$\text{Do–Fa} = \text{Do} \times 3/4$$

$$\text{Do–Sol} = \text{Do} \times 2/3$$

$$\text{Sol–Re} = \text{Sol} \times 4/3$$

$$\text{Re–La} = \text{Re} \times 2/3$$

$$\text{La–Mi} = \text{La} \times 4/3$$

$$\text{Mi–Ti} = \text{Mi} \times 2/3$$

In order to form another octave, all you need to do is double or halve any given string length.

This looks pretty neat and very simple, and most people were quite happy with this concept for a long time, but eventually someone came up with the idea of extending the scope of this scale. If you extend this scale to its twelve-tone conclusion by following twelve perfect fifths and making octave adjustments, the tonics never meet. In fact, they miss by almost a quarter of a half step. This inherent error at the unison, called the *diatonic comma*, makes this tuning system unusable as a twelve-tone system, since different keys are in and out of tune in different ways.

So, attempts were made to temper this tuning. A number of temperaments have been used throughout history, and in fact, some modern musicians continue to dabble with unusual temperaments, which may include more, or less, than twelve steps.

Many of these tuning systems using a greater variety of ratios were greeted with some success, but in the final analysis, it was found that all simple ratio systems fail to yield equal results in all of the keys.

Up to this point, all of the tuning systems were based on simple ratios. This was because these simple ratios represented the intervals we most enjoyed hearing: perfect fifth, perfect fourth, major third, minor third, and so on. All of these were expressed by simple fractions. But what would happen if these fractions were compromised just a little, so little that maybe we could not hear the difference, but enough to correct the diatonic comma?

This is the theory that leads to the twelve-tone equal-tempered system. The mathematicians knew that they needed a twelve-tone system because that was what musicians had been using for some time. They also knew that this new system would contain all of the intervals that musicians were used to hearing, but they would all be slightly compromised. Naturally, this new system had to begin to repeat exactly at the octave because the octave ratio could not be compromised.

Theorists let go of the super particular ratios and the need to have nice neat small fractions, and they came up with the concept of dividing the octave into twelve equal parts. Their attention was directed to the half step and the octave. Mathematicians already knew that pitch (in cycles per second) times two equals the frequency (in cps) up an octave. This is our simple 1:2 ratio. Now, in order to go from 1 to 2 in twelve equal steps, we need to find a number to multiply 1 by, successively twelve times, and yield the answer of 2. This number is said to be the *twelfth root of two*, and it can be used to obtain the size and location of all of the tempered intervals.

Frequency Comparison for Different Temperaments
(in cycles per second)

	Pythagoras	Mean Tone	12 Tone
A	220	220	220
A♯	234.932	229.879	233.08
B♭	231.77	235.397	233.08
B	247.5	245.967	246.94
B♯	264.298	257.013	261.63
C	260.741	263.181	261.63
C♯	278.438	275	277.18
D	293.333	294.246	293.66
D♯	313.242	307.459	311.13
E♭	309.026	314.838	311.13
E	330	328.977	329.63
E♯	352.397	343.75	349.23
F	347.654	352	349.23
F♯	371.25	367.807	369.99
G	391.111	393.548	392
G♯	417.656	411.221	415.30
A	440	440	440

Fig. 4.1. Frequency Comparison for Different Temperaments

The twelfth root of 2 is 1.05946; its inverse is .94387.

The twelve-tone equal-tempered scale is far from perfect. None of the intervals are in tune with the simple ratio scales of earlier times except the octave, but they are all close enough that most of our ears can make the compromise without discomfort. After all, we are flexible beings. What's most important is the fact that all the keys are equal and that all of the half steps are the same.

So, why is all of this important to us as bassists?

To begin with, it's nice to understand a little bit about where our language has come from. You can't know where you are going unless you are aware of where you have been. The discussion I have offered here is just the tip of the iceberg, in relation to this subject, and I recommend that any serious musician do some in-depth reading on this subject to better understand what we are listening to today. You can explore your recent roots or your most distant roots; in either case, there is so much to be gained.

You can also now see that the twelve-tone equal-tempered system is a compromise to the simple ratio systems. In fact, some of these ratio systems were not so simple. Most people will agree that the simple ratios are more natural, and as you will see in the next chapter, more in tune with the natural harmonic series. So, it is important to understand that there will be small discrepancies between tempered notes and notes derived from more natural ratios. These discrepancies can be heard if you listen carefully. On a fretted instrument, play the F#4 harmonic above the low F#2 on the D string. Now play the lowest F#3 on the G string. Can you hear the beating? Play the G4 harmonic just flat of the sixth fret on the A string. Now play the G4 harmonic located above the lowest C3 on the G string. Can you hear this as a unison? Temperament has taught us to accept these discrepancies. I believe that the acceptance of these discrepancies may be getting into our blood, and many of us have become too complacent about this subject. We all need to listen just a little more thoughtfully.

It is also a fact that any instrument built with frets utilizes all of this mathematical knowledge. The luthier uses the inverse of the twelfth root of two, .94387, to locate the frets in the twelve-tone equal-tempered system. String length times .94387 equals string length up a half step. If this is not adhered to exactly, your instrument will be useless, if you enjoy performing with other musicians.

In the early part of the twentieth century, A440 was generally agreed to be the international standard of tuning. In 1955, this standard was etched in stone by the Bureau of Standards. In earlier times, the pitch standard varied appreciably from place to place, and this caused much confusion. Luthiers were not sure how much string tension would be placed on their instruments. String makers didn't know what pitch their strings were going to be tuned to. Musicians could not be sure what pitch levels to expect if they traveled from city to city.

The standard of A440 was finally agreed to, and most people adhere closely to this standard today. Of course, rules are made to be broken, and many orchestras use an A slightly higher than 440. Some fixed pitched instruments are actually tuned to A442. But when one considers applying the equal tempered scale, the point of beginning is generally A440. This is a point of interest to all string players, as their instruments are tuned to open strings and consequently are tempered from those points, if they have frets. It is true that all modern-day stringed instruments have open A strings, and this point helps to keep string instruments close to equal temperament. More on this in the next chapter.

So, this is the system we live under. Most of us don't even realize that these constraints are there. Most of us don't think about all of these compromises taking place. Most of us have never considered having more than twelve notes in an octave or what would happen if intervals were different sizes from key to key, or what would happen if it was suddenly A447. Who really gives a hoot about Pythagoras anyway? Well, in a funny sort of way, you are related to him. Think of him as a great uncle or something.

Geometric Patterns

All conventional bass instruments referred to in this text are now traditionally tuned in a pattern of ascending fourths. This pattern of tuning has come about via much turmoil and happenstance, as was illustrated in chapter 1. The double-bass tuning pattern has gone through a metamorphosis of sorts and has settled to the E-A-D-G pattern. The electric bass, upon conception, merely mimicked the double-bass tuning (or the electric-guitar tuning of the lowest four strings, down an octave). In either case, the result was the same. Modern extended range instruments of five and six strings also utilize the tuning system of fourths.

It has already been stated that a number of varied tuning patterns may be used temporarily by the professional bassist as demanded by the music being performed. A few modern performers use unusual, and even irrational, tunings on a regular basis. But the fact is that the great majority of bassists, and string players in general, incorporate the same tuning pattern throughout their performance careers.

Although the tuning pattern of fourths is the accepted norm, what matters for most of us is merely the presence of some pattern. As humans, we have an inherent need for regularity, and patterns can be thought of as familiar, or regular, things.

Musical patterns come in many forms. There are interval patterns, scale patterns, chord patterns, sound patterns, and geometric patterns. Of all of these patterns, only geometric patterns are instrument-specific. They are formed because an instrument is what it is. Geometric patterns formed on a piano or a trombone are quite different from those formed on a bass. The fact that the double bass and the electric bass are tuned alike causes their left-hand geometric patterns to be similar, although their size is quite different. The geometric patterns give physical shape to our musical thoughts.

Geometric patterns are perceived in two ways. They can be *physically* sensed—that is, viewed or touched—or they can be *spiritually* sensed, imagined within the brain. Obviously, neither perception can take place without a great deal of playing experience. Through a long term commitment to practicing one's instrument, a clear vision of these patterns can be obtained. These patterns are a byproduct of the instrument we play, and in no way should they be

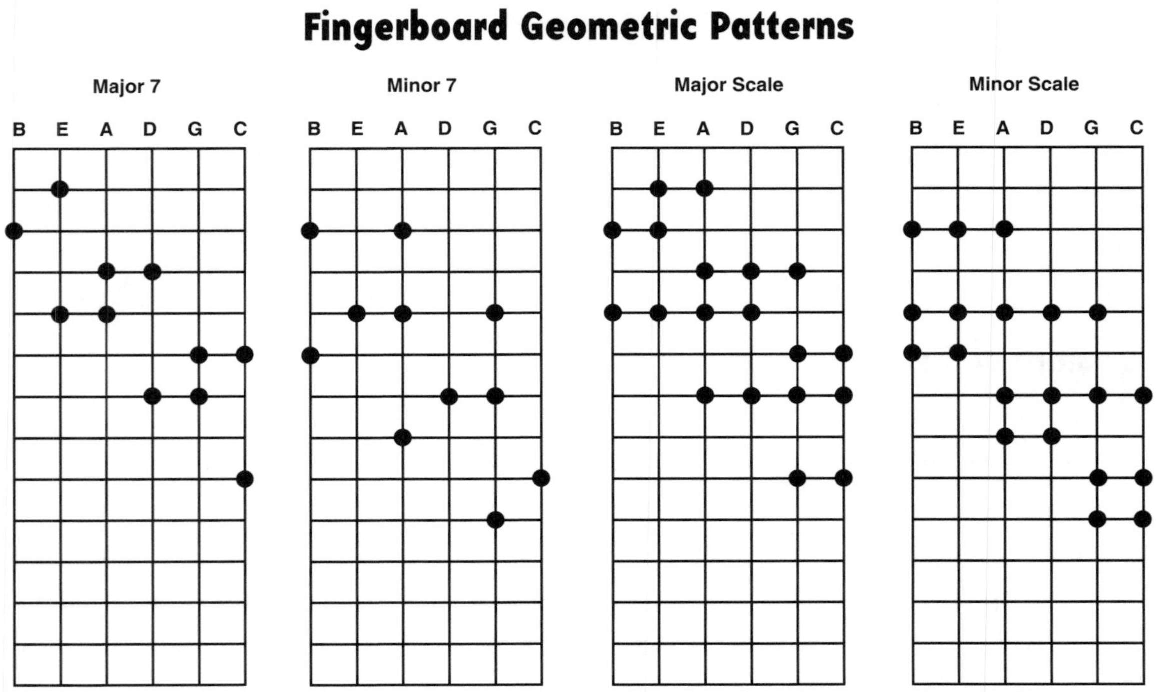

Fingerboard Geometric Patterns

Fig. 4.2. Major and Minor Arpeggio and Scale Geometric Patterns

considered musical entities. It is the responsibility of each player to understand the geometric patterns within his head and translate them to musical form. Otherwise, these patterns are useless jarbal.

Many bassists, especially fretted-electric players, first become aware of geometric patterns when they observe shapes as they watch their left hand perform repetitious work. These shapes are made clearer by the presence of the straight frets. Other players mentally sense the shapes initially while reading or otherwise performing while not looking at the fingerboard. These small shapes, initially seen as a lick or an arpeggio, are but minuscule pieces to a much larger picture. The inexperienced bassist must be careful to avoid narrow vision when first experiencing thoughts of these shaped patterns. It is imperative that all patterns be given musical meanings and seen as a part of the whole, the pattern of the entire fingerboard.

These geometric patterns are caused by the repetitious pattern of tuning. If the tuning pattern was non-repetitive, then the geometric patterns formed on the instrument would also be non-repetitive, and much more complex to understand. These patterns create physical shapes on the fingerboard that are ever changing with the music of the moment. These patterns can become large, complicated pictures to the well versed performer, and can enhance the performance within the mind of the performer.

Once performers can see this picture, they must draw it on the fingerboard. This drawing is done with the fingers of the left hand. In many ways, it is a sort of paint-by-numbers project. The fingers of the left hand can be numbered. The pitches being played can be given numbers related to their musical function. The intervals being created can be numbered and so on. The extent of this type of numbering is limited only by the imagination of the performer.

Each player must make the decisions as to which fingers to use to fill in the blanks or to connect the numbers. As the blanks are filled in, the picture is completed. The choice of fingers depends solely upon the painter's past experiences. Beginners put their fingers where they are told or just at random with unguided "no thought." As proficiency on the instrument is gained and self knowledge is achieved, performers can make their own choices about fingerings. These choices will glean thought and substance, for they are made through study and experience. When master status is achieved, a true understanding of the picture is known, and the highest level of performance can be presented. The master paints with guided "no thought" and in a style that all recognize and admire.

In order to come to guided "no thought," one must understand and spend much time with thought. Much effort should be put into fingering considerations. It is only through diligent studying and much consideration that players obtain the right to paint in their own manner and be able to return to the childlike state of "no thought" while performing.

Most players visualize patterns of the right hand also (see fig. 4.3). These are generally of a simpler nature, due to the fact that most conventional right-hand articulations can be expressed by using a system of 1 and 2. The human mind is very familiar with this yes/no or yin/yang nature of things, making right-hand articulations easier to conceive. This fact, however, does not relieve the player from long hours of practice related to articulation, for it is our touch hand that allows us the greatest capability of personal expression. Fingering possibilities of the right hand are further complicated by the addition of rhythm, articulations, and phrasing considerations.

Right-Hand Finger Patterns

Paradiddle

Roll

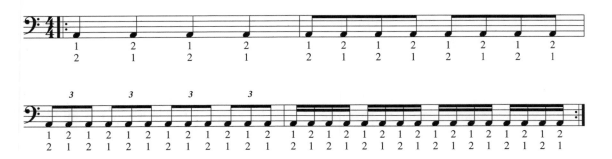

Fig. 4.3. Right-Hand Finger Patterns. Paradiddle and roll exercises applied to the two-finger technique of the right hand.

The great majority of electric players use either their index (1) or middle (2) fingers, or (usually the case) both. Double bassists do the same, although many more prefer using just one of the two. Further, arco strokes can be broken down to down bows (1) and up bows (2). The right hand does not cover physical space as does the left, so the visualization of a picture is much more of an abstraction. But the presence of a number of yin/yang type patterns stimulates the mind of the performer considerably and requires lengthy study.

CHAPTER 5
Harmonics

Theory

All vibrating strings produce *harmonics*, also called "overtones." When a string is set into motion, not only does it vibrate at the intended pitch (the *fundamental*), but other fractional divisions (*overtones*) of the string also vibrate within the whole. These fractional divisions vibrate as individuals, but are related to the fundamental—the lowest pitch in the series—and vibrate as parts of the whole. It is the entirety of all of these vibrations that makes up the sound and timbre we hear. The fundamental and all of its overtones are called *partials*, as each is a "part" of the overall sound.

Strictly speaking, the fundamental is not a harmonic, just a partial, but the fundamental is commonly referred to as a harmonic by string players, since it is part of the series of pitches produced by a vibrating string. In fact, the fundamental governs the harmonic series. Most theorists, however, do not consider the fundamental as belonging to the harmonic series. The musical understanding of the harmonic series, how it is constructed, and its usefulness to us as bassists, far outweigh the importance of the knowledge of any theoretical numbering approach to such a series.

All harmonics have two primary parts: points of no vibration or no sound called *nodes*, and points of maximum vibration or sound called *anti-nodes* or *loops*. It should be noted that a conventional pickup located at a loop gives strong volume to the vibrating harmonic, while a pickup located at the node of a harmonic would not sense its presence. It would still vibrate, but would be unheard through amplification.

All strings produce the identical series, or pattern, of harmonics, but the relative absence and presence of each partial determines timbre. Materials used in manufacturing strings may

Harmonic Series
(in cycles per second)

Function	Harmonic Number	Pitch
1	16	A5
7	15	G♯5
♭7	14	G5
6	13	F♯5
5	12	E5
♯4	11	D♯5
3	10	C♯5
2	9	B4
1	8	A4
♭7	7	G4
5	6	E4
3	5	C♯4
1	4	A3
5	3	E3
1	2	A2
1	**1**	**A1 (Fundamental)**

Fig. 5.1. Harmonics. These are the sixteen lowest harmonics produced when open A1 is sounded. The fundamental, A1, is counted as the first harmonic, in this chart. The harmonic number is listed in the center, the function related to the fundamental is listed on the left, and the pitch is listed to the right.

accentuate certain harmonic registers. Of course, string gauge and tension also affect tone. These factors account for the different tonal qualities associated with different brands of strings on any given instrument.

The physical locations of the loops and nodes within a given harmonic can be found by simply dividing the string into the appropriate number of equal parts. If we consider an open A string as our starting point, dividing the string in half yields the second harmonic, A2. The three nodes are located at the bridge, at the nut, and halfway up the string. The two loops are located halfway between the nodes. If we now divide the string into thirds, we have the pitch E3. The four nodes are located at the bridge, at the nut, at the 1/3 distance, and at the 2/3 distance. The three loops are again located at the center points between the nodes. Dividing the string into fourths yields A4, and so on. The fundamental is usually the strongest partial. As the partials rise in frequency, their relative strength generally diminishes, though this is not always exactly true, due to the numerous variables involved.

All of the higher harmonics are naturally in tune with the fundamental by means of simple fractional ratios such as 1/2, 1/3, 1/4, 1/5, and so on. But since we relate to other instruments

Placement of the Most Common Natural Harmonics

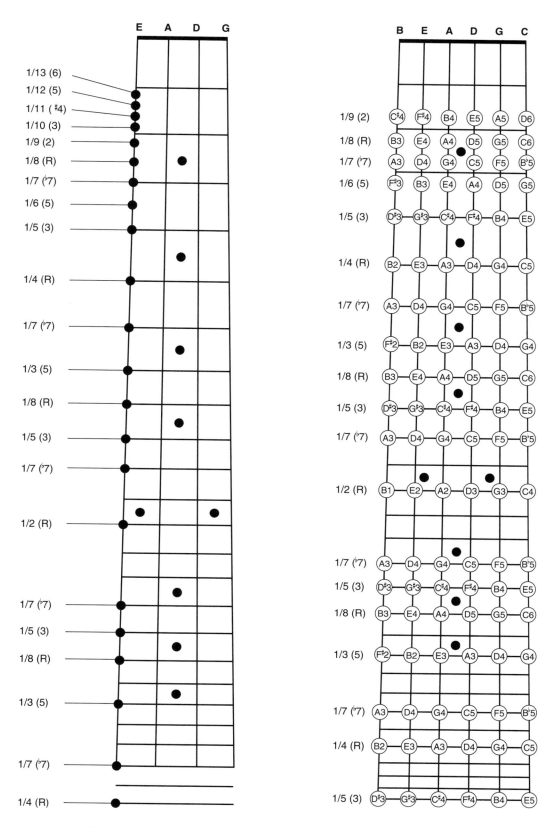

Fig. 5.2. Nodes of the Most Common Natural Harmonics. Simple interval relationships to the open strings are shown in parentheses. To the right are the pitches produced at common harmonic locations.

by means of the twelve-tone equal-tempered system (no simple ratios exist, just the twelfth root of two), a number of intonation discrepancies can be found when comparing the natural intonation of harmonics to the man-made system of equal temperament. Fortunately, these discrepancies are usually so small that our ear accepts them as true.

Physical actions such as adding mass and tension to a string can affect the entire harmonic series and how in tune we perceive it to be. More on this in chapter 6.

If a player wants to cause a harmonic to vibrate alone, the loop and node locations must be known. When the string is lightly damped (with the left hand) at a node, and plucked or bowed at or near a loop, the harmonic can be heard, separated from its fundamental and the rest of the series. It is actually heard as a new fundamental. This action must be light and precise in the left hand, and strong and pointed in the right.

Common Use

Relative Intonation

Double bassists and fretless players use harmonics as an aid to performance intonation. When performing alone, or with no other instruments providing pitch references, harmonics can be used, along with open strings, as intonation reference points. These reference points are non-movable and will be in tune if the instrument is in tune. Consequently, the use of these reference points helps the player to stay in tune.

Consequently, the use of these reference points helps the player to stay in tune when playing closed notes. When using a harmonic as an intonation reference, it is best to find divisions of octaves or fifths from the closed notes being referenced. These intervals are the easiest to identify aurally, being the most consonant. Intonation decisions must be made quickly, so consonant intervals are best suited for this purpose. Of course, some harmonics are out of tune with our tempered scale and are not well-suited to be references. Knowledge of the harmonic series, intonation awareness, and performance experience will help you to decide which harmonics work best as intonation aids.

False Harmonics

The harmonics that are produced by the open strings are referred to as *natural harmonics*. They occur as natural byproducts of the open strings. If we close a string, an entirely new set of harmonics, unique to the newly closed string, is produced. These are called *false harmonics*. Their availability for use is limited due to our own physical constraints; our left hand is busy closing the intended note.

A. String Closed with Finger

B. String Closed with Thumb

C. String Closed with Right-Hand Thumb

Fig. 5.3. Methods of Closing Strings to Play False Harmonics.

Many false harmonics can be performed by closing the string with one finger and reaching to a node with another finger of the same hand (see fig. 5.3a). The note can also be closed by placing the hand above the fingerboard and using the thumb. This approach allows for a greater reach up the fingerboard (see fig. 5.3b). It is also possible to touch a node with the thumb of the right hand and pluck with the index or middle finger (fig. 5.3c).

Although proficiency with false harmonics is not considered necessary for everyday playing, a knowledge of how to find a given pitch may prove helpful one day. Just remember that you can apply the harmonic series to any note and you can physically measure the fractional divisions of any closed string.

Intervals, Colors, and Chords

Harmonics can be used to create a number of interval and voicing combinations. Closed notes can be combined with harmonics to create thousands of intervals, colors, and chords, but there are limits and constraints as to what can be performed with harmonics.

Many voicings that include natural harmonics are not playable by the use of false harmonics. The fact that we have but five fingers, without endless reach, limits our ability to combine many pitches.

Accurate Tuning Procedure

The most widely accepted manner of tuning the bass is by the use of harmonics (see chapter 6). Although this method is not perfect, it affords the bassist a quick and easy way to achieve predictable results with each tuning. Most people cannot detect the small discrepancies left unattended by this method.

To sound a harmonic, lightly touch the string with a left-hand finger at a harmonic node, and pluck or bow the string with your right hand. Once the harmonic sounds, quickly remove your left-hand finger to allow the harmonic to continue to sustain. This action frees up the left hand to turn the tuning machines during tuning. The left-hand finger need not be removed so quickly if you are using a bow, since the bow forces the note to sustain. When you can clearly sound harmonics, you will be able to tune your instrument as outlined here.

Of course, you can sidestep listening to yourself by using an electronic tuner, but it is imperative that you learn to tune by ear. The process of listening to yourself and thinking about the pitch relationships as you tune is an ongoing joy for all of us.

First we tune our A string to A440. Most players play either the octave harmonic of A110 or the harmonic above the fifth fret, A220. If you can tune to A220 from a keyboard, you may find this easier, but get used to A440. It is what you will usually be given in a professional situation, and it is the point around which our twelve-tone system is tempered.

Once you have the A string tuned, match the A3 harmonic on the fifth fret to the A3 harmonic on the seventh fret of the D string. Then, match the D4 harmonic on the D string to the D4 harmonic on the G string. If you are tuning a 4- or 5-string, tune the E string by matching the E3 harmonic on the seventh fret of the A string to the E3 harmonic on the fifth fret of the E string. Tune the B string by matching the B2 harmonic on the seventh fret of the E string to the B2 harmonic on the fifth fret of the B string. If you are tuning a 6-string, tune the C string by matching the G4 harmonics located at the fifth fret of the G string and the seventh fret of the C string.

All of these harmonics must be tuned beatless, and it is always a good idea to check and double-check your work. Beating is the sensation that we perceive when two pitches are close, but not quite in tune. All beats must be eliminated for the unisons to be perfect. Take all of the time required to do a perfect job.

As you tune, you exert and release tension on the neck, causing small movements that may affect strings already tuned. Instruments being restrung or having been far out of tune will need numerous checks.

Many beginners tune by matching unisons of open strings with closed notes at the fifth fret one string below. This method works for a fretted electric but is useless on a fretless or double bass. It is also true that the unisons do not project the clarity that the harmonics possess, consequently allowing for

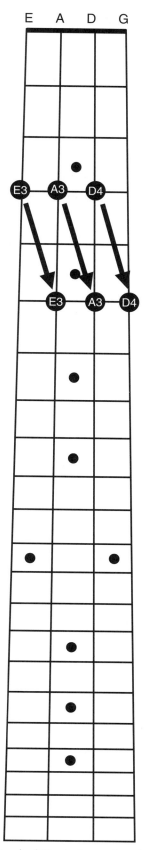

Fig. 5.4. Standard Way to Tune a Bass by Using Harmonics.

larger mistakes. A mistake of one beat at the unison is four times greater than a one beat mistake at the harmonic up two octaves. More on beats in the next chapter.

The order of tuning the strings presented above is my own personal preference. The only non-variable is that the A440 (or 220) must be used. This can be accomplished by tuning the A3 harmonic on the D string initially and matching it to the A3 harmonic on the A string or vise versa. From here, you can proceed up or down first; it's your choice. It is, however, important to establish a pattern that you will always follow. This is tuning, not personal expression. You want to get as perfectly in tune as quickly as possible, so a habitual process is most useful.

CHAPTER 6
Setting the Intonation

All other adjustments should be completed before setting the intonation of an instrument. Adjusting string height or neck bow after setting the intonation may cause your intonation to be untrue, forcing the need to repeat the intonation setting process.

There are a number of electronic tuners available today, and they are all quite capable of helping you to intonate and tune your instrument. With a quality tuner, you can actually accomplish this task without listening to yourself. Observing someone tune or intonate their instrument without listening to it has always bothered me, and I have personally avoided using electronic tuners for this reason. When I speak of intonating an instrument, I am referring to the setting of the string lengths so that the pitches are found at the precise, proper locations on the fingerboard. This process should not be confused with the tuning of your instrument each time you pick it up to play.

Electronic tuners are most useful to the average player in performance situations that make it difficult to clearly hear your instrument, making it difficult to tune up. They are also useful in the orchestra pit, affording the player the ability to retune without being heard during dialog or otherwise quiet moments. It is my opinion that, whenever possible, it is more desirable to tune your instrument by ear.

Under normal playing conditions, the best use for a tuner is to establish the A440 necessary to tune the instrument. This can also be accomplished with a simple tuning fork, and you won't need batteries. Most players actually match the A440 to the A220 harmonic above the A110 on the D string.

Many players also find the tuner a useful tool in perfecting performance intonation or working on ear training during practice time. Intervals can be performed, tuned by ear, and then compared to the precision reading of a tuner. For this purpose, a tuner can be an excellent learning and practice tool.

A high-quality tuner will actually display readings in fractions of cps and will greatly simplify and speed up your task of setting the intonation, but this is an expensive tool that most performers could do without. It is most useful to the technician who must intonate many instruments each day.

The time spent intonating an instrument by ear is valuable, as it affords you time to listen very carefully and evaluate the exact sound of your instrument. I highly recommend that you learn to tune and intonate your bass without the aid of a tuner. You will truly enjoy what you hear.

With all of these ideas stated, I will now discuss intonation with no more mention of an electronic tuner. Purchase one, if you must.

Double

The double bass is not constructed with the intention of the intonation being adjustable. The mere fact that there are no frets or position markers present makes it theoretically impossible to set the intonation, as the player sets the intonation with each note performed. It is possible, however, to change the string length to a certain extent, thus moving the relative placement of the pitches on the fingerboard. This action will rarely be supported by the original luthier, as each instrument is constructed according to a strict set of measurements, and the speaking string length is one of these measurements. But many players have performed small string-length adjustments with agreeable results.

Measure the string length of five or more different styled basses. You will find that the string length is rarely the same from one instrument to another. Generally, the standard string length of 3/4 and 7/8 size instruments is between 40 and 43 inches, with most instruments falling in the middle of this range. The 5/8 size instrument's string length is in the 38-inch range. As mentioned earlier, the string length is determined by the bridge location, as the nut is stationary. This bridge location is theoretically determined by the center cuts in the *f* holes.

This range of string lengths exists, in part, to accommodate our hand sizes. String lengths of greater than 43 inches become difficult to negotiate for players of average size. The length is also kept relatively similar from one instrument to another to abide by general standardization practices, thus making it possible to perform on different instruments with a minimal amount of adjustment to one's playing technique. Finally, the length of string is necessarily long to clearly produce the low pitches with rich tone. If the player decides to alter the intended string length, all of these factors will be affected to some degree.

The most common manner in which to adjust the string length is to move the location of the bridge. This action can best be accomplished with the instrument on its back and the strings loosened. After adjusting the bridge location, you must adjust the soundpost in the same direction. This could mean that you will need to shorten or lengthen the post to fit the inner body contour in its new location. To shorten the post, sand or saw it until it is the right length. Make sure that the ends of the soundpost fit the inner contour of the front and back. If the post is too short, a new one will need to be fashioned, since you cannot add length to a post. As you tighten the strings, once the new post is positioned inside the bass, be sure that the bridge remains standing erect.

Very small adjustments can yield big changes in sound output, sometimes nice, sometimes not so nice. You may need to make several adjustments to discover that you should have left the instrument alone in the first place. Have a clear vision of the intended results of any adjustments such as these before embarking upon a useless journey.

It is also possible to slightly adjust the angle or location of the bridge by gently tapping it with a rubber mallet or book while the instrument remains strung up. The double bass bridge is oftentimes unwittingly bumped and dislocated slightly. A gentle tapping can easily relocate a slightly askew bridge. If you are tentative or fear cracking the bridge, this action is best left to someone with previous experience in the maneuver.

String length can also be permanently altered by installing a false nut. A false nut is not really false or untrue. It is simply located in a place that is not intended by the original design of the instrument. A false nut is generally installed up the fingerboard from the original location, so as to shorten the strings. The act of shortening the strings will affect the output of the instrument, but it cannot always be predicted in what manner. No adjustment need be made to the bridge location when a false nut is installed. You can experiment with the location of a false nut by using a capo and retuning the instrument to match open strings to the capoed notes.

One of the reasons one chooses an instrument in the first place is the playability, and the string length is an important factor in judging playability. An instrument with a string length that does not suit the owner or that the owner cannot adjust to may be better sold than altered. Most bassists prefer to avoid making adjustments such as these.

Fretted Electric

The presence of frets, small deviations in the size of certain instrument parts caused by seasonal changes, and all of the variables caused by the numerous types and gauges of strings available today, create the need to individually intonate each string of the fretted electric bass. Once intonated, unfortunately, the job is not completed. Factors that may require you to reintonate include continued seasonal changes, heavy wearing of the strings, replacing the strings, subsequent action adjustments, and the wearing of the frets due to normal playing. Some of these factors occur over a long period of time and others may occur quickly. Let your keen ear tell you when your instrument needs to be intonated, and do not delay your action.

As I mentioned earlier, all action adjustments should be completed before attempting to set the intonation. Raising or lowering the strings, or adjusting the neck bow, affects the intonation. Performing these adjustments after setting the intonation may require you to intonate the instrument additionally.

If every bassist lived where the weather never changed, used the exact same brand and gauge of strings, and set their action exactly the same, there would be no need to set the intonation. The manufacturers would be aware of our needs, and all instruments could be constructed to play in tune under the conditions in which we would all be living. But this is obviously not the case.

The frets are placed in permanent positions on the fingerboard, but seasonal changes and neck bow manipulation (through truss rod adjustments) can cause small physical expansions or contractions in the instrument's length. This movement can actually move the fret location relative to the saddles, causing small changes in the length of each vibrating string. We have already learned that frets are carefully placed in locations coinciding with twelfth-root-of-two measurements, but these placements will all be wrong if the string length is not adjusted to match the individual needs of each instrument.

In addition to this "movable fret" problem, there are a number of small intonation problems associated with any given set of strings.

Our great uncle, Pythagoras, set forth some interesting theories about vibrating strings, which come to bear on our intonation needs. In a nutshell, he stated that the perfect vibrating string would be infinitely long, have no mass, and have no tension. Of course, all of these suppositions are impossible, but remember, he was a mathematician and viewed the world in the numerical sense of perfections. He further explained that as a given string is shortened, fattened, and tightened, it slowly loses the qualities of perfect vibration. It is easy to see that the electric bass has short, fat, tight strings compared to Pythagoras' perfect string. So how does this affect our intonation?

All of these qualities—short, fat, and tight—are relative and must be viewed as such. Our E string is fat relative to our G string, but it is thin relative to out B string. All string lengths become shorter and relatively tighter and fatter as one moves up a given string.

You may find that certain locations on your instrument produce intonation discrepancies that cannot be completely corrected. The major culprit we now call *enharmonic distortion* is what Pythagoras discovered. Enharmonic distortion occurs in relatively short, fat, and tight strings. The relative shortness, fatness, and tightness cause the harmonics of a given note to distort sharp and out of tune when struck or bowed. Oftentimes, the pitch will settle to be more in tune as it is allowed to sustain. The stronger the attack, the more accentuated this problem will be. The inability to adjust performance intonation, due to frets and to the shorter strings of an electric bass, compared to a double bass, makes this problem most prevalent on the fretted electric bass.

You can easily hear enharmonic distortion in the upper register of the E and B strings, and if your instrument has more than twenty-four frets, and you use medium or heavy-gauged strings, you might perceive this out-of-tuneness at the top of your higher strings as well. Compare your G2 on the E string to your open G2. Can you hear the beating of the harmonics? Compare your G3 on the D string to the closed G3 on the G string. Maybe you can detect slight beating even here.

What can you do about this unsolvable problem? Setting your action within the range intended by the manufacturer and paying attention to the seasonal changes of your instrument is a start. Instrument and string manufacturers are well aware of these inherent intonation problems and are always looking for better ways to compensate for them. Quality strings and fine instruments generally leave you with but small problems to solve. Maybe you will need to avoid the upper register of your E string on solo passages. Perhaps you will need to practice your shifting a little more in depth so you will be able to shift away from this area more effectively. If you perform a great deal in the upper register, you might consider lighter gauge strings. These intonation discrepancies caused by enharmonic distortion are small. They usually go barely noticed, if the instrument is set up correctly and intonated properly.

So now, onto setting your intonation. I will present two methods, both of which can be accomplished by ear, but you must learn to listen carefully. All you will need is a screwdriver or Allen wrench to adjust the saddle screws, A440, and your ears to give you direction. Check out the screw that runs from the tailpiece through the saddle, and be sure that you have a screwdriver that fits it comfortably. You do not want to strip this screw, so a good fit is essential. All we need to do now is tighten or loosen this screw. Tightening it will lengthen the string, loosening it will shorten it. Most electric basses have a saddle equipped for each string. Some older models have one saddle for two strings. These instruments cannot be intonated as precisely as the modern instruments that have one saddle per string. For this text, I will consider that the instrument has one saddle per string.

Standard Approach

It's a good idea to rough out the tuning first, before getting into the fine-tuning later on. Set the length of your G string to the length dictated by the scale of your instrument. A long-scale instrument should have a string scale of 34 inches. Check with the instrument builder, if you are unsure as to the correct scale.

Measure the string's length from the fingerboard side of the nut to its contact point on the saddle. This is the speaking length of the string or the scale of the instrument. Adjust the string length as necessary to match the suggested measurement by tightening or loosening the saddle screw. It is always best to start in this position even though you will rarely leave the string at this exact length. The scale is theoretical, and seasonal factors—neck bow, shortness, fatness, tightness, and some others not yet mentioned—will all come into play in determining this length. The manufacturer is aware of all of this information but does not have total control, due to all of the variables that the owner adds. The final word is left to you by means of the string length adjustment. After setting the G string's length, set the lower strings' lengths, each progressively a little longer than the one before. This extra length will help to compensate for the string width problem associated with the lower strings and for the increasing tension as these fatter strings are closed. Generally, the added length gets greater as you proceed from the D string to as low as the B string. Compensation on the D string is a twist or two, maybe 5 mm. Compensation on the B string should be three times this distance or more. It is best to set the starting distance of a C string to match the G string.

We are setting these distances before we begin tuning to save ourselves work later on, as this is the configuration that most instruments will adhere closely to when the intonating process is complete. Our process of setting the intonation from this point on is considered fine tuning and requires careful listening. If you like, you can skip this initial step, but you will spend more time on the other steps later in the process.

Once the individual string lengths are generally set to the lengths designated by the builder, you must tune your instrument as carefully as possible, making sure that all of the strings are as precisely in tune as you can get them. Tune all of the unison harmonics to be completely beatless as outlined in the previous chapter.

Fig. 6.1. Usual Shape of Electric Bass Bridge. Thinner, higher-pitched strings are generally shorter when the bass is intonated correctly.

With the instrument's open strings in tune, we start by intonating the G string. We already know that we have the pitch D4 as a harmonic above fifth fret of the D string. The harmonic D4 is also located above the seventh fret on the G string. Another node of this harmonic is above the nineteenth fret of the G string; in fact, at this location, the harmonic and the closed note are the same pitch. These are the pitch locations that we use to intonate all but the lowest string.

Firmly play the D4 harmonic on the fifth fret of the D string, and quickly play the closed D4 at the nineteenth fret of the G string. You must hear these pitches sounding together, and they must sound as a perfect unison. Be sure that you are pressing against the D4 at the nineteenth fret of the G string with an even pressure that is not too great. Also, be sure that you do not bend this note. Bending the note or pressing too hard will give an untrue initial reading. If this unison is in tune, you can move on to the next step. If not, you must determine how it is out of tune. Remember that you are comparing a closed note to a harmonic. The harmonic is a product of the D string, so we consider it in tune and our point of reference. You must decide if the closed D4 is sharp or flat of the harmonic D4. If the unison is way out of tune, it may be easy to hear the direction of error. If the pitches are very close to perfect unison, it may be very difficult to determine whether the closed D4 is sharp or flat. Listen for the beats. If the beat rate is clear and slow, the pitches are close to unison. Play the unison again, and try bending the closed note or pressing harder against the fret this time. If the beat rate gets faster, then the closed note is sharp. If the beat rate slows down, then the closed note is flat.

When you have made your judgment of sharp or flat, you will need to adjust the string length accordingly. If the closed note is sharp, lengthen the string. If the closed note is flat, shorten it.

If the string is more than about 5 beats per second out of tune, loosen it a little to relieve some tension before making your adjustment (no need to break a string doing your intonation). In all cases, adjustments should be made gradually—that is, a turn or two at a time. With experience, you will learn how much length adjustment is needed.

After adjusting the string length, retune the G string to match the D string by the usual use of harmonics.

Then repeat the entire step, and continue repeating it until the unison is perfect. Essentially, the three pitches of D4 must match. First, match the D4 harmonics on the D and G strings. Then, match the closed D4 on the G string with the D4 harmonic on the D string. Continue adjusting string length, retuning, and matching until you are satisfied with your results.

On occasion, the unison may be so close that it is impossible to decide which direction the error is in. Do not fret. Just make a guess, and turn the screw. If you are wrong, the problem will be more noticeable. If you were right, you just got lucky.

With the G string set, proceed to intonating the D string. Tune the instrument as usual, using harmonics. Strive for perfection each time you tune. You will employ the exact technique used for the G string on the D string, but using the A3 harmonic above the fifth fret of the A string and the A3 harmonic (and closed note) at the nineteenth fret of the D string. Remember that the G string is set. Do not adjust it unless you need to start over.

After the D string is set, go on to the A string. Always save the lowest string for last. If you are intonating a 5-string, do the B string after the E string. If you are intonating a 6-string, do the C string before the B string. Always remember which strings you have completed and which are still in need of intonating.

The lowest string presents a special problem when you use this technique of intonating. We have been matching a pitch from the nineteenth fret of one string to a unison harmonic produced from the string just below it. There are no strings below the lowest string, so we must change our technique.

You must first observe the geometric shape that your saddles are creating. Consider where your lowest string would fit into this shape visually and place it there. This placement will, in most cases, be close to the final location of the saddle.

Let us consider intonating the E string. As always, tune the instrument carefully. Now, you must go about checking unisons and octaves from the E string to the others that are already intonated. Play low G1. Does playing this note cause your open G2 to vibrate by itself? This is called a *sympathetic vibration* and is an indication that these two notes are close to being in tune. Check the D2 on the E string with the open D string. Are these in tune? If not, what happens when you press the note harder or bend the note? If this brings the note into tune, the string must be shortened. If the intonation gets worse, you must lengthen the string. Check the G2 on the E string with your open G string. Allow the notes to settle, as you may perceive enharmonic distortion at this location. Does the open G string begin to vibrate by itself? You must use what you hear to determine whether the length of the E string needs manipulation. Proceed to play across the entire instrument, listening very carefully to the consonant intervals of fifths, tenths, octaves, and so on. Like intervals should sound similar. If you are happy with your intonation, walk away. Check it again in a week or so to be sure you heard it correctly.

You can check your closed E2 on the E string with the E3 on the G string, but you may not be happy with what you hear. If you have very perceptive ears, you may hear some other things that annoy you when playing with a perfectly tuned keyboard. If you can concentrate on beat rates, there will be some intervals that just don't seem right. You may find some spots on your bass that you just can't get in tune no matter what you do. Well, it's okay, I suppose. Or at least, it's normal.

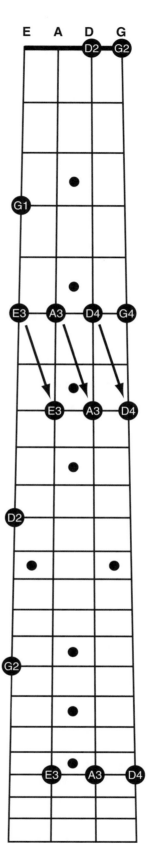

Fig. 6.2. Location of Notes and Harmonics Used in the Standard Technique of Setting Intonation.

Earlier, I mentioned twelve-tone equal temperament and how there are no nice, small, logical fractions involved in this system. I also mentioned that the harmonics were products of nature and were based on nice, neat, small, logical fractions. So, how can we play in tune in the twelve-tone equal-tempered system, using a tempered instrument, but tuning by the use of non-tempered harmonics?

This is a complicated question that deserves some discussion here and much consideration on the part of the performer.

The most important single thing that our system of tuning and intonating, and our intonation system, need to accomplish is repetition at the octave, or in-tune octaves. Of course, we need to understand all of the intervals that we hear, but remember, small compromises usually go unnoticed. If there is not repetition at the octave, we will be presented with new intervals, as we hear notes of more that an octave apart, and this will not go unnoticed. This repetition is accomplished, but only on a per-string basis. Since the frets are placed on the fingerboard by use of the twelfth-root-of-two ratio, any octave that is found using separate strings is slightly flat. Using this tuning method, we also find that none of the other intervals are perfectly in tune, but most are acceptably close and acceptable to our ear.

So, can you tune a tempered string instrument with frets by use of a non-tempered system and achieve perfect intonation? Well, not exactly. There are discrepancies that warrant further study.

We have already discovered a number of physical problems that can cause small intonation discrepancies: string tension, string tightness, string height, string fatness, neck bow, enharmonic distortion, and now tuning by use of harmonics when playing in the twelve-tone equal-tempered system. All of these factors cause small deviations. Instrument manufacturers, string manufacturers and now the owner, in setting the intonation, have all made attempts to solve these intonation problems, but there will exist small deviations that cannot be reconciled when tuning beatless by harmonics and playing in the twelve-tone equal-tempered system on a fretted instrument.

Remember that we just intonated the instrument matching harmonics to closed pitches on adjacent strings as unisons. This means that the fifths created would be perfect if played as harmonics but would be slightly tempered if fretted. Fretted fourths would be perfect if played on adjacent strings because the frets are straight, but they must be tempered just a little sharp in the twelve-tone system. In fact there are more wrong frequencies than correct ones using the technique outlined here.

Open String Frequencies
(in cycles per second)

	Intonated by Standard Approach	Intonated by Tempered Method
B	30.94	30.87
E	41.25	41.20
A	55.00	55.00
D	73.33	73.42
G	97.78	98.00
C	130.37	130.81

Fig. 6.3. Open String Frequencies

Since we tuned to A440, and we have an open A string, this string and all of its tempered fretted notes are in tune with the twelve-tone system. Looking at the D string, its tempered open pitch should be 73.416 cycles. When tuning by harmonics, we get the frequency of 73.333. We know that the A3 on the D string is in tune, since we matched that note with the open A string. But every note between D2 and A3 is slightly flat, the flattest being the open D2. Any closed notes above A3 will be slightly sharp, with the sharpness increasing as the pitch rises.

Similar problems can be found on the G string. The closed A2 on the G string is about 109.76 cps when it should be 110. D3 on the G string is close to 146.65 cycles. By our tuning system, it should be 146.83 if tempered correctly. The open G, when tuned using harmonics, is 97.777; it should be 97.999.

On the E string, we find open E1 is 41.25 cps by our tuning and 41.203 by temperament. Closed A1 is about 55.07 cycles; it should be 55. It is 55 on the A string.

Generally speaking, one finds that all of the pitches on the D and G strings, up to the nineteenth fret, are slightly flat of their twelve-tone tempered counterparts, with the fretted pitches above the nineteenth fret becoming sharp. All of the lower pitches on the E string veer just sharp of the correct positions. As stated earlier, the pitches on the A string are correct.

If so many of these pitches are out of tune, why do we use the system of intonating? Because it keeps the octaves in close tune and is easy to manage. Upon listening to the discrepancies that I have pointed out, it is quite difficult to detect them under the best of listening conditions. After all, we are only human. These discrepancies are very small.

However, if the instrument is not kept in tune and is not correctly intonated, these discrepancies can multiply and become very noticeable, even to the average listener. So, it is important to understand all of these factors that come into play when intonating the fretted electric bass in this manner.

Tempered Approach

You can intonate your instrument to match the twelve-tone equal-tempered system more precisely than as with the standard approach, but you must be prepared to listen much more carefully. You need to perceive the beating of harmonics that are slightly out of tune and detect their relationship to time, much as a piano tuner does. This is not an easy process, and it requires much practice and patience. Most players are satisfied with the standard approach, but I have outlined the tempered approach for those that are bold and striving for perfection, for surely, if you can follow this process, you will be able to hear the difference.

When we hear two pitches sounded together that are not quite in tune, we perceive beats. The two frequencies move through space, and since their periods are not quite equal, their wavelengths oppose each other at regular intervals. Essentially, the node of one and the loop of the other occasionally cross, and at this point, we hear no sound. So the beating that we hear is the regular alternation of sound and no sound.

This beating is related to time, and since frequency is measured in cycles per second, we measure beats in *beats per second*. The pitches of 97 and 98 *cycles per second* (cps) sounded together will beat once each second, the pitches of 440 and 441 cps sounded together will beat once each second. Since this relationship is constant, we can use a perceived beat rate to determine frequency if we know one frequency.

By finding the open pitches produced when tuning with harmonics using Pythagorean math, and comparing these with the necessary frequencies required by the twelve-tone equal-tempered system, we can do our own math, and find beat rates to use for our adjustments. Then, we only need to adjust our open strings.

When calculating a beat rate for use in this process, we must remember which way to make these adjustments. The A string is always correct and need not be tempered, as long as we tune to it to A440. (If you tune to another pitch on a different string, an entirely new set of calculations would be necessary.) All strings above A must be tempered sharp, and those below must be tempered flat.

When beat rates are very slow, we need to express them in terms of a longer length of time than one second. A beat rate of .2 per second is difficult to deal with, but by expressing it as

Frequency Per String
(in cycles per second)

	Standard	Tempered		Standard	Tempered		Standard	Tempered		Standard	Tempered
E	41.25	41.20	A	55.00	55.00	D	73.33	73.42	G	97.78	98.00
F	43.70	43.65	B♭	58.27	58.27	E♭	77.69	77.78	A♭	103.59	103.83
F#	46.3	46.25	B	61.74	61.74	E	82.31	82.41	A	109.75	110.00
G	49.05	49.00	C	65.41	65.41	F	87.21	87.31	B♭	116.28	116.54
A♭	51.97	51.91	C#	69.30	69.30	F#	92.39	92.50	B	123.19	123.47
A	55.06	55.00	D	73.42	73.42	G	97.89	98.00	C	130.52	130.81
B♭	58.34	58.27	E♭	77.78	77.78	A♭	103.71	103.83	C#	138.28	138.60
B	61.81	61.74	E	82.41	82.41	A	109.88	110.00	D	146.50	146.83
C	65.48	65.41	F	87.31	87.31	B♭	116.41	116.54	E♭	155.21	155.56
C#	69.37	69.30	F#	92.50	92.50	B	123.33	123.47	E	164.44	164.81
D	73.5	73.42	G	98.00	98.00	C	130.67	130.81	F	174.22	174.61
E♭	77.87	77.78	A♭	103.83	103.83	C#	138.42	138.59	F#	184.58	185.00
E	82.5	82.41	A	110.00	110.00	D	146.67	146.83	G	195.56	196.00

Fig. 6.4. Frequency Per String. "Standard" means intonated using standard harmonics. "Tempered" means intonated using the tempered approach.

1 per five seconds, it is easier to understand. All the beat rates we must deal with are small and best related to larger intervals of time than one second. It will be quite useful to have a timepiece that displays seconds for use as you learn this method.

Begin by tuning the instrument by use of harmonics as usual. Start with the A3 harmonic on the A string. Tune this beatless to the unison A3 harmonic on the D string. The D string must be made sharp so as to produce .248 beats per second, or 1.24 beats per five seconds, or 1 beat per four seconds.

Proceed in tuning the other strings using the temperament chart given (see fig. 6.4). Never retune the A string. Always quadruple-check your work, especially when first learning. With some practice, you will be able to do this without thought.

When you can tune the instrument by use of this tempering system, you can go about intonating it just as you did before, by matching the notes on the nineteenth fret to the harmonic above the fifth fret of the next lower string. The process is exactly the same except that each time you tune up the instrument, you must remember to temper each string.

This process should yield intonation that is closer to the intended perfect result, but never lose sight of all of the other variables that affect intonation. All of the physical factors mentioned in this chapter affect your ability to obtain a perfectly intonated instrument. You may need to temper your tempered approach to achieve the intonation that you are looking for. Fretless and double bass players may also wish to try this tempered approach of tuning the instrument, for all of your open strings, bar one, are slightly out of tune with the twelve-tone equal-tempered system, if you tune using harmonics.

So, in theory, this is the best system of intonating and tuning that I have found, and you may possess the ability to hear the difference. You may be satisfied with the standard approach, insisting that it works fine. This is okay; this is where most players are. You may try this tempered approach and dismiss it as too much hassle for the small divergence that it yields. You may decide not to be bothered with any of this nonsense, and take your bass to a technician to be intonated, or use a tuner every time you tune and intonate, not even hearing it, but rather watching the display needle. The choice is yours. Remember, we listen to music.

Fretless Electric

As with the double bass, the fretless electric bass theoretically cannot have its intonation set due to the absence of frets and the player's need to intonate each individual note when performed. There are, however, a number of considerations that warrant careful attention to the adjustment of the string length. Adjusting the string length by manipulating the saddle does not actually adjust the intonation. Rather, it determines the exact locations of the pitches on the fingerboard.

The fretless electric bass may have fret markers or position markers on the front of the fingerboard, and almost certainly has side position markers on the neck. The presence of these markers creates a visual relationship to which the player may become dangerously attached, or at least, keenly aware. Many players actually place their fingers in pitch locations using their sight rather than using their ears. For most players, the best method of determining intonation is a combination of the two, but it is imperative to be able to negotiate the fingerboard without the use of your eyes. Clubs and orchestra pits are sometimes dark. When reading, the performer may be allowed only random glances at the neck. It is for these reasons that the performer must not rely upon seeing the instrument.

The player, however, cannot avoid observing the fingerboard during many performances, and indeed, the visual relationship can help to finely tune and accelerate the thinking process, under many circumstances. It is for this reason that the precise setting of string length is done. If we are going to see the pattern of notes, we should see it displayed correctly. Of course, each instrument has an intended scale, or string length. This distance should be adhered to closely, since the luthier intended this distance be used, as it is one of the many numerical calculations needed for proper construction.

To set the proper string length, first determine the intended scale of the instrument. For most electric basses, this is 34 inches, or long scale. If you are unsure of your instrument's scale, contact the manufacturer.

Since there are no frets, other visual references aid our fine-tuning the string length. The G string should first be measured and set to the scale of the instrument. For a long-scale 4-string bass, set the G string to 34 inches. For an extra-long-scale 6-string, set the G string to 36 inches.

Each lower-pitched string is made slightly longer to compensate for the increasing fatness of these strings. This compensation can be as little as 4mm and as much as 13mm. A high C string can actually be slightly longer than the G string, but it is generally very close in length to the G string, depending on gauge. All of this presetting is as outlined under "fretted," above.

After setting the string length in this mechanical manner, play the octaves of each string. If your instrument has fret markers, your finger should close this note just on the left side of the marker so the point of contact is right on the marker. If there is no fret marker, refer to the side marker; it should be just sharp of your finger. Then, check the G string with a ruler. Exactly half the distance of the entire string scale should be the distance to the octave. The other strings will be slightly off, due to the fatness compensation.

Now, with the instrument carefully tuned, play over its entire range slowly. You must listen to the pitches carefully. Check as many unisons, octaves, and double octaves as possible. Use your knowledge of harmonics and how we intonated the fretted electric bass to help you. Look at where the notes lie when they are in tune. The physical relationship of the notes should be consistent throughout the entire range of the instrument.

Side markers should be placed in the same geometric locations as fret markers. Consequently, all notes should lie right on top of fret markers and/or side markers. Finger placement should be just flat of these positions so that the point of contact is at the markers. If the note location/marker relationship is not uniform over the fingerboard, more length adjustments are necessary. If note locations tend to get sharp of the markers as you move up the neck, the strings need to be made shorter. Conversely, if the note locations go flatter of the markers as you ascend the string, the lengths must be made longer. The note locations should form a straight line, or theoretical fret, across the fingerboard.

If there are no positional markers present, precise string length is not so critical, and it need only be made comfortable to the feel, within the intended scale of the instrument.

When you are pleased with the string lengths, set the instrument aside and walk away. Come back later, and repeat the process of carefully tuning up and playing slowly with careful, attentive listening and checking. If you are happy, recheck yourself in a week or so after a number of performances. Once the intonation is set correctly, you should only need to make small adjustments in the cases of altering the gauges of your strings or after seasonal climate changes.

CHAPTER 7

Fingering and Positions
of the Left Hand

One of the areas of greatest concern to bass players is the technical fingering facility of the left hand. Left-hand fingering ultimately determines overall facility on the instrument. In general, natural physical constraints of the left hand far outweigh those of the right hand, causing the left hand to be most performers' technical limiter. There are several reasons this is so.

The fact that about ⅘ of the population is right handed is the single greatest cause of deficiency in left-hand technique. Additionally, many players are what I call very right handed; that is, they are just plain clumsy with their left hand. These inborn right-handed tendencies force the player to devote extra practice time to the physical development of the left hand.

The left hand is what I call the "work hand." The constant closing of strings against the fingerboard is an arduous physical task. In performance situations, there is often little or no time to rest, as playing can be continuous. Even simple music can be physically difficult for the left hand to perform. Consider twenty-four measures of low F1 whole notes. Consider playing a simple repeating riff for fifteen minutes while other players come and go soloing. Then, it's time for the bass solo! Most music involves more active left-hand movement. Consider those up-tempo solo sections. The bass player must play every chorus; each soloist plays but a few. Consider the bass parts Beethoven wrote. What was he thinking? Whether playing one note or flying through 32 in two measures, the strain on the left hand is constant—especially if the strings are fat and the action is high!

All of this continuous specific work is centered on individual fingers and their supporting physical structures. Although the muscles that operate the fingers can become quite strong through regular conditioning, they remain small in comparison to most other muscles in the human body. As I discuss in chapter 12, these smaller muscles, and the connecting tissues that work directly with them, can break down or become injured if not properly conditioned and cared for. The inordinate amount of work required of the left hand of the bassist creates an area of concern that must not be overlooked, if a long prosperous playing career is your goal.

As I mentioned earlier, right-hand articulations tend to be strokes of 1 and 2, or up and down. Even seemingly complicated right-hand patterns can usually be broken down into simple opposing strokes like those of a computer. This is not true of the left-hand movements. The need for the regular use of more than two fingers, the crossing of strings, the relative location of the hand on the fingerboard, the variations of possible fingerings, and the phrasing of the music, all cause the ultimate fingering of the left hand to become a seriously complicated dilemma.

The size of the average human hand has guided much of our concept of fingering in the past, but today, professionals recognize more and more that traditional fingering styles can be modified to better suit performers with hands of differing sizes. Actual hand and finger size is a strong factor when determining a fingering approach, but should not be considered by the beginner. The beginner has not yet attained the knowledge necessary to make a logical choice related to this or any other performance-related subject. This knowledge can only be gained through guided experience.

When considering which fingering approach to use, it is not the approach that is as important as the effort expended by the player that ultimately guides in the development of fine technique and musicianship. The act of learning and studying a method brings discipline to your playing, even if you later decide to modify or abandon the course of study. It is through study that performers gain the right to make their own decisions. Beginners place their fingers in locations that are comfortable and convenient, giving no thought to what they are doing, playing their strengths, and making no effort to improve their weaknesses. In so doing their playing has no meaning. Students study and consider the fingerings, they practice and perfect them, and they must think about them to get them right. Their playing is growing and has a purpose. Professionals place their fingers in the locations that they have predetermined to be correct with no thought. They have earned the right to perform with no thought by studying and thinking previously. Their performance is natural, effortless, and filled with meaning.

Allowing your left-hand fingering to be haphazard is a death sentence to your development as a competent bassist and musician.

Double

There are a number of fingering and positional methods considered usable on the double bass. The most commonly used method of fingering is taught in both the Simandl and Nanny methods. These are the most widely used methods at present. The numbering of positions differs slightly in these methods. In fact, different editions of the Simandl method display different position numbers, which adds to the confusion.

Left-hand position refers to fingerboard locations at which the hand plays across with no shifting up or down. It is important to remember that the actual naming or numbering of positions is a learning tool and is not as important as identifying musical, or key-related, uses for positions.

Position numbering is started at the nut, the lowest position being called the *half position*. As the hand is shifted up the fingerboard by half steps, new positions are formed and given various names, depending on the method being studied. These actual position names are meaningless. My favorite teacher, David Cobb, once told me that there were three positions on the bass: half position, first position, and emergency! He was, of course, poking fun at all the bassists who are hung up on memorizing position names rather than musical ideas, and the fact that it is difficult to perfect shifting into higher positions.

Most method books teach positions starting at the nut and moving up the fingerboard. The advantage of this are that the player learns the lowest notes first. This lower register is used the most by the average bassist, it seems logical to start at the open strings and move up in pitch, and it is easy to teach a beginner reading in conjunction with this method. The disadvantages are that the widest reaches are in this area (making initial playing and intonating very difficult), the fingers fit half steps more naturally up the fingerboard about five to seven half steps, the tuning harmonics are not located at the bottom of the fingerboard, and players can develop a fear of shifting, or "heights," if they initially linger in the lower positions too long.

With all of this said, it is best to find a competent teacher and procure the method book that he or she recommends. Follow the method from beginning to end, striving to understand and emulate the thoughts presented through the guidance of your instructor. After considerable study, seasoned players are able to make the adjustments, if any, needed to suit their own physical needs and playing style.

Left-hand fingering is a much more complicated issue than that of the positions. Both the Nanny and Simandl methods present excellent examples of standard approaches to fingering of the left hand. Proper, predictable, and regular fingering will be a great aid in attaining good intonation.

A. 3-Note Position   B. Intermediate Position   C. Thumb Position

Fig. 7.1. Double Bass Left-Hand Positions

Standard fingering allows for three pitches to be located on each string in any given position in the lower portions of the fingerboard. These pitches are closed with 1, 2, and 3–4 fingers. The use of 3 and 4 together is necessary to achieve the correct reach for proper intonation, and to achieve enough strength to hold the string down as necessary (see fig. 7.1A). This fingering is recommended up to the octave, but many players begin to use 3 alone in the area as they pass from the ordinary position to the thumb position (see fig. 7.1B). Once at the octave and in full thumb position, it is recommended that you use T, 1, 2, and 3. Your 4 will not reach the fingerboard without considerable adjustment to technique, so it is not normally used in the thumb position (see fig. 7.1C). In the thumb position, the fingers can easily reach half or whole steps, and in some cases, can accommodate larger distances, without shifting, as the player moves well up the fingerboard.

This issue of fingering can become very complicated and requires much individual attention to hand comfort, intonation, natural ability, and musical demands. All of these needs are best studied with an experienced and trusted teacher.

Electric

Electric-bass positions are more standardized than are double-bass positions. To begin with, there is no half position. All of the positions simply coincide with the fret numbers: first fret, first finger is first position; second fret, first finger is second position; third fret, first finger is third position, and so on. This system extends all the way up the fingerboard.

Fig. 7.2 Electric Bass Four-Note Positions

The standard fingering approach for electric is also more straight forward than is double-bass fingering. Since the instrument is smaller than the double bass, most players can reach four pitches in all of the lower positions using fingers 1, 2, 3, and 4 (see fig. 7.2). This adds a half step to each position of the electric bass, as opposed to that of the double bass in positions below the octave (twelfth fret). Upon reaching the area of the octave, it is possible to extend the positions by half or whole steps, depending on the reach of the player.

Many players use double-bass fingerings in the lower positions so as to avoid fatigue in the left hand or just to make the reaches more comfortable (see fig. 7.3). The four fingers cover three frets, with the ring finger usually doubling the pinky. This practice, which I call "cheating," is particularly useful on fretless to achieve correct intonation. Players with slighter hands also find this modification useful. This is one case where cheating is okay.

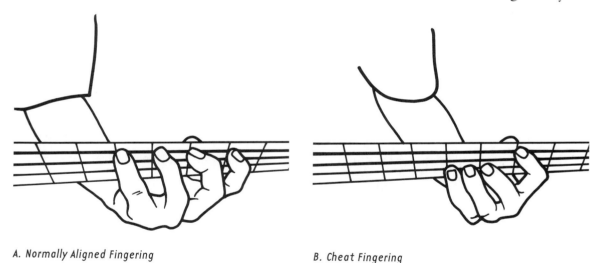

A. Normally Aligned Fingering   *B. Cheat Fingering*

Fig. 7.3. Double-Bass Fingerings on Fretless Electric. Lines are drawn to indicate where frets would be located.

A number of players use stretch positions to avoid or lessen shifting. Stretch positions incorporate skipping frets within a position by extending the fingers (see fig. 7.4). This is not recommended to the novice or even the average player, as it places additional strain on the fingers, makes for poor intonation on fretless, and causes players to avoid working on their shifting. Shifting is the most difficult aspect of bass playing, and avoiding its practice is like preparing to run a marathon by walking 26 miles.

Fig. 7.4. Electric-Bass Stretch Fingering

Position and fingering variations are also possible by pivoting, or swiveling, from the left thumb. The thumb is generally opposed to the fingers in a position between the index and middle fingers. By pivoting the hand so that all of the fingers are extended away from the thumb, a greater reach can be achieved without shifting the thumb. This type of movement can be utilized when playing back and forth between several positions quickly, or repeatedly, in the lower positions, but can best be used in the upper register to greatly extend the reach and melodic range with minimal arm movement.

The left hand has a number of other functions, beyond simply closing notes.

1. **Muting.** Muting can be accomplished in two ways by the left hand. On fretted electric, place your finger on top of the fret so that half of it is on the speaking side of the string. The meat of your finger acts as a damper and greatly reduces the sustain. At the same time, it removes any brilliance from your tone. You must be very precise with your finger placement. If you miss flat, you will not dampen the string. If you miss sharp, the string will buzz, or you will close the next note up!

   On fretless, you must use less fingertip and must press the string with more of the meat of your finger. I call this playing *flat fingered*. At the same time, you need to lighten your grip just enough to allow your finger to act as the damper, while not releasing so much as to lose contact with the fingerboard. This technique also requires precision of touch.

2. **Harmonics.** As I discussed in chapter 5, harmonics are produced with a light touch of the left hand. The left-hand fingers need to be light and accurate (see fig. 5.2). Perfect coordination with a strong right-hand stroke is essential to producing a strong sound.

3. **Stopping Over-Ring.** *Over-ring* is the sounding of notes that have not been plucked. The most common cause of over-ring comes about when harmonics of low strings begin to vibrate as you play notes on higher strings.

   If you play A2 on your G string, and then suddenly dampen it, you will hear the pitch A2 still ringing. This sound is coming from your A string. The harmonic A2 produced at the octave of the A string has been forced into vibration by your playing of the A2 on the G string. This is called a *sympathetic vibration*.

In itself, this does not sound bad, but if you play the same A2 on the G string and next play B♭2 on the same string you will hear the half step of A2, from the octave of the A string and B♭2 on the G string.

Most players solve this dilemma by damping the A string with the right-hand thumb, but damping can also be accomplished by use of left-hand fingers, if they are available. This is an advanced technique, since your left-hand fingers may be busy when you need them. You must also identify the locations on your bass where over-ring is a problem. Look for notes on higher strings that are roots or fifths of your lower strings. These are the greatest offenders.

4. **Barring.** *Barring* can be accomplished on electric by pressing your finger flatly across two or more strings. This action can be used to play notes located on the same fret quickly. Barring takes a great deal of strength and can be quite painful if your fingers are not up to it. I prefer to use separate fingers whenever possible to conserve strength.

Barring can be of particular use to the 6-string player in the upper register. Many beautiful chord voicings are available in this register, and having the ability to bar is of great use to the 6-stringer.

Barring on fretless is less common, as it is quite difficult to bar across several notes and keep them all in tune.

5. **Bending Notes.** Bending notes is accomplished by closing the note, plucking it, and pulling or pushing the string with the left-hand fingers. Most players prefer to pull the string, as this is a stronger motion than pushing is.

On fretted instruments, notes can only be bent sharp, since you cannot go below the fretted note. On fretless, you can start flat and bend up to pitch. In order to bend up to pitch on fretted, you must start a full half-step flat.

Bending notes is much more common on guitar, but all great bass players use this technique to some degree.

6. **Vibrato.** Fretted players can simulate vibrato by rolling their fingers between frets or by rapidly, gently bending notes. This is not a true vibrato, since the pitch variation cannot go below the note due to the presence of the fret.

Vibrato is most useful to the fretless player for intonation adjustments and to add emotion to the music. The note should be closed as accurately as possible, and then the left-hand finger is rocked to produce the desired effect. It is important that vibrato is not used to cover up a player's lack of good intonation skills. Vibrato is an addition to competent playing, and competent playing includes good intonation.

7. **Dead Notes.** *Dead notes* are notes played for their percussive value only. The exact pitch of these notes is not articulated. Dead notes are produced by touching the string at the desired location with a left-hand finger and plucking with the right. Care must be taken that you do not touch at a harmonic node or a harmonic will be produced. To avoid this, you can place two or more left-hand fingers on the string so that the harmonic does not sound.

Dead notes are particularly prevalent in funk and jazz. In notated music, a dead note is usually indicated using an × for the note head. It is located on a pitch, but you don't always need to articulate the note at the exact location indicated.

8. **Position of the Left-Hand Thumb.** If you watch a number of electric-bass players, you will notice a number of different styles of placing the left-hand thumb. Generally speaking, the thumb opposes the index and middle fingers. It should press against the back of the neck and arch inward for maximum use of hand strength. If you are watching from the front, it is best not to be able to see the thumb tip.

As I mentioned, there are a number of variations on this position, and certain musical passages may cause you to adjust your thumb position. The position I have outlined here makes the best use of your natural hand strength in most circumstances.

9. **Shifting.** Shifting is a complex subject, and I consider it to be the most difficult task to master on the bass. Players who neglect the practice of shifting are avoiding one of the most fundamental skills demanded by the instrument.

A shift is defined as moving the entire hand from one position to another. The thumb must move during a shift. The warm-up exercises in figure 10.1, for electric, are excellent examples of shifting exercises. You can create many exercises such as these with a little imagination and some professional guidance. Be sure to strive for accuracy of finger placement at all times.

Since the electric bass is still an infant, there is a limited amount of written material available for use as a method. The teaching literature that is available is quite varied in scope, and in general, lacks standardization and general acceptance. It may be many years, if ever, before standardization is achieved in relation to the technical aspects of the electric bass. As with the study of the double bass, serious players should seek out an experienced professional to aid in their development.

CHAPTER 8

Tone Production

There are a number of factors to be considered when determining how to physically affect tone production. The same pitches located on different strings have different timbres, due to the differences in string length, tightness, and fatness. Differences in pickup readings at various nodal locations can also affect note timbre. Acquaint yourself with these variables, and be aware that they fluctuate from bass to bass. Choose where to finger a note primarily for musical reasons, and secondarily for physical comfort. Play the notes that sound the best, not the ones that are easiest to reach. Always try to find musical logic behind your fingering choices.

Where you attack the string also affects the overall timbre. Plucking close to the bridge yields a thin, pointed sound. Bowing in this area yields a loud, shrill tone. Both sounds are weak of the fundamental. Moving the fingers or the bow toward the fingerboard increases the presence of the fundamental and produces a much fuller sound. General bowing is done at about 1/6 to 1/7 of the total distance of the vibrating string from the bridge. This general location is the average point of articulation for most electric players too. Many electric players find their plucking locations by the physical locations of their pickups. Resting your thumb on or near a pickup anchors your hand and provides physical "landmarks" that you can find without looking. Fortunately, the pickups are usually located in the 1/6 to 1/7 distance range. Experiment with different locations of plucking and arco playing, always bearing in mind the desired end result.

Professional guidance is often necessary to obtain optimum results regarding these issues.

In considering tone production, it is useful to isolate the instrument and your hands to further study a number of the variables.

Double

Right Hand

• Pizzicato

There are four basic pizzicato techniques available on the double bass. If you watch your favorite players closely, you will be able to categorize their particular techniques into one or more of these.

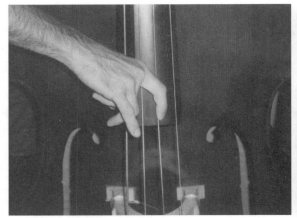
A. One-Finger Pizzicato (Jazz)

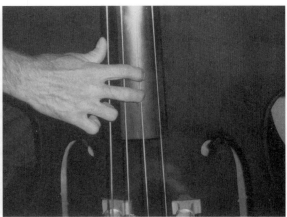
B. Two-Finger Pizzicato (Jazz)

C. Classical German (Traditional)

D. Classical French (Traditional)

Fig. 8.1. Pizzicato Positions

The jazz pizzicato is played with the sides of the fingers near the bottom of the fingerboard. For play in the lower register, this distance is generally ⅕ to ⅙ of the vibrating string's distance from the bridge. Many jazz players use only the index finger, but a number of players additionally use their middle finger to augment the sound produced. The middle finger can be used separately or to support the index for a particularly strong sound. The jazz pizzicato is the strongest of the bass pizzicatos, as the power of the stroke is generated at the wrist, often causing the entire hand to be involved in the stroke. By using the sides of the fingers, the player can get more meat in contact with the string. This accentuates the fundamental of each note and adds even more to the power of the stroke. Additionally, the power of the stroke can add a percussive attack, giving the pitch more definition. The amount of finger surface that comes in contact with the string can extend from the tip to the second knuckle, but it is usually one knuckle long. Once this broad area becomes callused, there is little chance of developing the dreaded blisters.

The traditional (classical) pizzicato must often be performed while holding the bow. Classical music often calls for the player to switch from arco to pizzicato very quickly, so the player must be able to pluck the strings while holding the bow in the same hand. The stroke is accomplished with either the index or middle finger; some players use either or both. The finger is placed perpendicular to the string with the elbow at a 90-degree angle, and the string is pulled perpendicular to the fingerboard using the entire arm, keeping the finger joints relatively taut. The point of attack is generally located at about a quarter of the vibrating string's distance from the bridge. The sound is deep and not very pointed, due to the location of the pluck. The plucking location should be kept near a loop of the lowest harmonic to accentuate the depth of tone. The string should not hit the fingerboard unless indicated in the music. The timbre of this stroke must match that of the other members of the violin family, as in orchestral music, the entire string section often performs pizzicato simultaneously.

The electric style of pizzicato, as applied to the double bass, uses the index and middle fingers in a plucking motion powered at the joints of the fingers. This style of pizzicato is very similar to the traditional finger-style stroke used on the electric bass. Articulation location depends upon the desired timbre and ranges between ¼ and ⅙ of the vibrating string's distance from the bridge. The thumb can be used to anchor the hand to the fingerboard, and the point of plucking is above the end of the fingerboard by one to six inches or so. After plucking, the fingers generally come to rest on the string below, enhancing speed and dampening open strings. Since the amount of finger coming in contact with the string is limited to the tip, timbre quality can be quite pointed. It is difficult for most players to generate a large amount of volume with this stroke, since it takes a great effort from the fingers, but players using this style generally use an amplifier to increase volume.

• Arco

Most bowing is done from the shoulder, with the elbow joint kept relatively stiff and straight. Fast passages, ornaments, and the like incorporate wrist and hand movement. Proper consideration must be paid to these basic principles of bowing, as good quality sound cannot be developed without proper physical form. The arco technique is best studied with a master.

Tone production, when performing arco, is governed by four basic factors. There are no exact rights and wrongs related to any of these factors, but there are a number of finite characteristics that should be considered.

The type of hair and the bow's tension (tightness) affects your ability to produce a smooth sound. Horsehair comes in many colors and textures, and you must decide which variety is best suited to your style of playing. Also experiment with the tightness of the hair. Loosen the bow hair after each performance. Leaving it tight adversely affects the hair and the spring of the stick. An experienced player is able to sense the tightness of the hair through viewing the bow or playing a note or two. The novice may need to touch the hair to feel the tension. Keep dirt and body oils from getting on the hair; these interfere with the hair's ability to grab the string. Touch the hair as little as possible, and clean your hands before playing whenever possible. By counting the number of screw turns that are required to tighten your bow hair, you can loosen by the same amount, thus eliminating the need to physically touch the hair in checking its tightness. Bass-player etiquette dictates that you never touch the hair of another player's bow.

Bow pressure and bow speed are major variables in determining the sound and volume of any given note. In general, increased pressure will increase volume, and bow speed needs to be increased with the rise of pitch.

There are upper and lower limits to pressure. At too light a pressure, the fundamental pitch is lost and harmonics or just string noise are produced. At too heavy a pressure, string slashing and quacking, distorted notes may be produced.

Bow speed not only relates to the pitch produced but also to the physical characteristics of the string, its composition, length, tension, fatness, and so on. If you play whole notes of equal volume, moving directly up the string, each proceeding note will require a little more bow speed. But if you play this same example, crossing strings whenever possible, the bow speed will decelerate slightly each time you cross to a higher string. This is caused by the variations of tension, length, and fatness encountered as you cross the strings.

The seasoned player realizes that bow speed and bow pressure work together to produce the intended timbre and pitch, and that during performances, one cannot devote much thought to these actions. Much time must be spent in the practice room perfecting one's touch on the instrument so that it becomes second nature, guided without thought during performances.

Lastly, the right hand needs to be steady. There are needs for light, firm, heavy, easy, and any number of other strokes. These strokes require much varied ability of the right hand, but they all have one thing in common: steadiness. We laugh about music sometimes and say, "It's not brain surgery," but the steadiness of hand of a brain surgeon is quite useful to the bassist, as the steady right hand governs the clarity of tone produced.

Left Hand

A strong left hand aids in good tone production. The firm contact of the string against the fingerboard is essential for pitch clarity. Weak fingers, a fatigued left wrist, or bad technique can result in inadequate note closing, leading to string buzzing, string muffling, and missing notes altogether. It is essential that the double bassist's left hand be kept in top physical form at all times. Much care must be taken to promote individual finger strength and independence along with mobility of the wrist. The bassist should pay careful attention to his ability to perform using proper biomechanics in this area.

Electric

Right Hand

There are three common ways to articulate the electric bass (see fig. 8.2). These are the finger style, slap, and tapping. Not included in these, but still used by some players, are the use of a pick and plucking with the thumb. Pick playing is much the same as on guitar, only

A. Finger Style

B. Slap/Pop

C. Right-Hand Tapping

Fig. 8.2. Finger Styles for Electric Bass

the majority of the plucking is single-note up and down strokes. Thumb plucking was used in the 1950s and 1960s. It was lost for twenty years, and came back in the 1990s with the addition of the thumb-heel mute and the popularity of 5- and 6-stringed instruments.

Standard finger style makes use of the index and middle fingers, although it is possible to use the third finger in place of one of these or in addition to them. Most players can accomplish the job with the first two fingers, and this is considered the most common means of plucking the electric bass. The thumb can be used as an anchor, a guide, or a mute, as the fingers move across the strings. Plucking is done with the fingertips as *down strokes*, where the finger comes to rest on the string below, or as *up strokes*, where the finger plucks in an upward motion and remains in the air after the stroke. In either case, finger alternation is done as the music dictates. The player must make every effort to keep the fingers used at equal strengths so as to equalize alternating strokes and create versatility of technique.

Slap incorporates two strokes: a right-hand thumb *hammer* or *slap* stroke, and a *pull* stroke, with one or more fingers. The slap stroke is usually executed just at or below the base of the fingerboard. This stroke is much like the stroke of a piano hammer and can originate at the base of the thumb or in the wrist. The pull is accomplished by placing the finger below the string and pulling upward or outward. These actions cause the string to slap against the frets, generating the characteristic sounds. It is interesting to note that slap bass originated on the double bass and was made popular by players such as "Pops" Foster (with Louis Armstrong) and Wellman Braud (with Duke Ellington) in the early to mid part of the twentieth century. A New Orleans style bassist named Bill Johnson claimed to have invented slap bass when his bow broke on a gig sometime before 1920. Many modern-day double bassists still pull this slapping trick out of their bag, from time to time.

Tapping is accomplished by closing the desired pitches on the fingerboard with a rapid, strong stroke of the fingers of the right hand. This powerful stroke simultaneously closes the note and causes the string to vibrate. A tapping variation can be accomplished by slapping the fingers of the left hand down to produce a similar effect. Serious tappers combine the two for a marvelous effect.

These styles are not mutually exclusive. Most present day players mix and match them to suit their needs and desires. Many songs incorporate more than one articulation style, so professionals should acquaint themselves with all available styles.

Left Hand

As with the double bass, electric bass players' left hands must attain and maintain the strength necessary to guide them through any performance without physical limitations.

This does not mean that they need to play as fast as possible for as long as possible. As players mature, they become aware of their own potential in relation to their circumstantial needs. Students work at proper technique, building muscle bulk, and accomplishing tasks that were impossible in the past. Mature players know what is required of them and what they are capable of doing. They also have goals of things they have yet to attain. The left hand must possess the strength and agility to allow all of this development to take place in a reasonable fashion, as dictated by musical requirements. Players must direct much attention to the strengthening of the left hand.

Low-Interval Limits

You may wish to play two or more notes together, forming an interval or chord structure. When performing multiple notes, you must consider the register of the notes you are choosing. Randomly playing low notes together can often produce rumble or "thunder," rather than the desired intervallic effect.

Most harmony and arranging books include a section on low-interval limits. A low-interval limit is the point below which an interval no longer sounds clearly like the interval it is intended to be. This confusion of sound is caused by the lowness, or wave size, of the associated pitches and the beats generated by them. Intervallic beats become slower as you go lower in pitch. The interval of C2 and E2 will beat half the speed of the interval C3 and E3. As beats become slow enough to discern clearly, the problem begins. As bassists, we need to be concerned with these aural limitations so that we do not mindlessly perform intervals or chords that cannot be understood by the listener.

My low-interval table does not mimic those that I have seen in theory books, but rather is compiled through my own experience. Experiment with interval combinations and chords, and decide for yourself what the lowest acceptable location of each interval might be.

When combining more than one interval to form a chord or hybrid structure, the location of the lowest violation dictates the lowest allowable location for that structure. All upper-octave adjustments have the same limit as their lower octave counterparts. That is the low-interval limit of a M2 = that of a M9, the limit of a P4 = that of a P11.

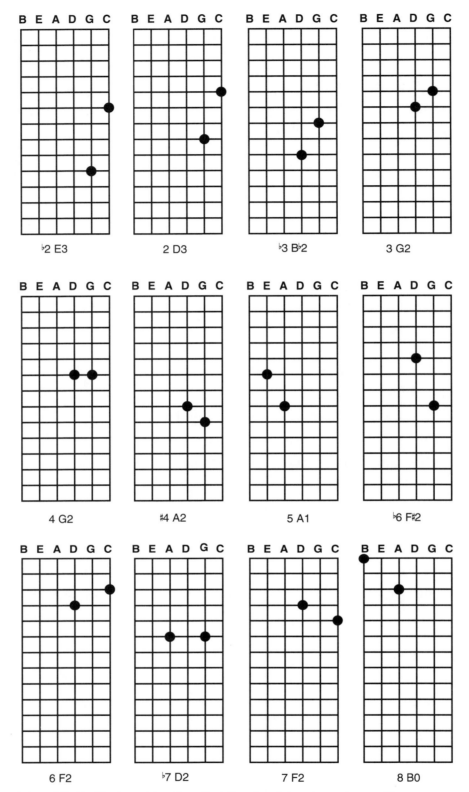

Fig. 8.3. Low Interval Limits. The lowest locations that the given intervals are discernable.

CHAPTER 9
Special Considerations for 5- and 6-Stringed Electric Instruments

---

Instruments with more than four strings accentuate some of the problems that a 4-string player negotiates every day. The special considerations that arise due to the addition of strings can be particularly bothersome to players who double between 4-string and 5- or 6-string, since they often are forced to adjust their mental and physical approach to the instrument. An extended-range instrument also demands a much more flexible musical approach from the performer, and the performer needs to be aware of this.

Musical Considerations

Upper Register

The bassist's bread-and-butter work is playing bass lines. Whatever the style of music, there is always a bass line and a bass player to play it. Many bassists are soloists, but still, the bulk of their work is playing bass lines.

With the addition of the C string to the electric bass, the range of the instrument is heightened dramatically, and much of this new upper register can be reached with minimal shifting. Numerous chords can be performed, as there are now enough upper-register strings to construct clear voicings. This is a wonderful addition to the bass, but the performer must carefully consider the function of the newly added upper register.

Most music books define the bass register as from E1 to around E3. This register can also define the register of bass function. *Bass function* can be defined as the establishing of the tonal foundation upon which the harmony is built. It is often root function, and in most ensembles, the low to mid melodic range of the bass establishes the frequency range of bass function. The E1 is determined by the traditional lower limit of the conventional bass. This

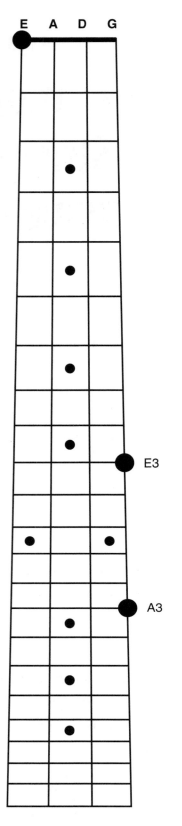

Fig. 9.1. Functional Register. The bass's functional register extends from the bottom of the instrument to E3, with an extension to A3 possible.

note can be extended down to whatever note is the lowest available, but the E3 defines the upper register of bass function and cannot be raised by much without sacrificing depth of support. It is true that bass parts go above E3 quite often, but this is the extreme high end of the register. Material in this register is often soloistic in nature or supported from below by additional notes. A3 is the extreme upper limit of the bass register. These notes between E3 and A3 are what I consider "color notes" of the bass register, and they do not legitimately perform bass function.

Considering these facts, and the fact that the upper register notes are physically easily performed on electric basses (since they follow the same pattern of tuning as the lower), the bassist must be careful not to sacrifice bass function for the addition of midrange and upper-register melodic material. The bassist must control the urge to mindlessly play across the instrument with careless disregard for register constraints. Performing bass lines in too high a register does not provide proper foundation in any style of music, and it suggests unsupported sound.

If intending to perform a bass line on an instrument with a C string, the bassist must learn to augment the lower register with the addition of upper register activity and explore the lower positions in depth. Bass function must not be carelessly omitted due to the selfishness of the performer.

In addition, 5- and 6-stringed instruments often have extended upper registers, making each string two octaves or more. The notes in the extreme upper register of such instruments are susceptible to enharmonic distortion, much as the high strings of a piano are. These strings are short, tight, and relatively fat, causing the enharmonic distortion.

This distortion can cloud up chord intonation or interfere with the intonation of unison parts. Lighter-gauged strings relieve enharmonic distortion to some degree, but lighter strings sacrifice low-register gusto of tone. When facing this problem, players must evaluate their particular needs and compromise accordingly.

Lower Register

Extending the lower register of the electric or double bass gives enhanced depth to the instrument. Today's sound equipment does a wonderful job of reproducing the extremely low register of the bass, and more and more bassists are performing on 5- and 6-stringed electrics in order to gain access to this register. Although it is not as common, double bassists have been performing on 5-string basses and instruments with E string extensions for centuries. All bassists in major orchestras have extensions or 5-strings.

The inherent nature of very low pitches causes the bassist two areas of special consideration. Low notes are more difficult to hear than higher pitches, and extreme low notes tend not to be as melodic as higher ones. The sheer size of the wave lengths of these very low notes causes these phenomena. A 36-foot wave can only move so fast, and perceiving it takes a little more time than your typical 2-footer.

Bassists must be careful not to let their playing habits override these acoustical facts of life. Fast parts performed on the A and D strings may sound like soup when performed an octave lower on the B and E string. Melodic lines are clearer to the ear if performed above the extreme low register.

The lowest register of the extended-range bass is best used for support. Chord roots, octave-supporting parts, and pedal points are good examples of musical uses for the lowest register. Of course, there is always the occasion for a special effect. Any bassist who has played Beethoven's Sixth Symphony knows first hand the effect of playing these low notes quickly. Beethoven was writing a part for a thunderstorm.

There is another musical low-range problem that relates to 5- and 6-string electrics. The relative fatness of the B string causes enharmonic distortion to creep down the string into the usual playing register. Enharmonic distortion can begin to be detected around D2 on the E string of most electric instruments. The problem is perceptible below this point on most 5- and 6-string electrics with a low B string, commonly approaching G1. The notes located up the B string also tend to be very boomy. This fact also relates to the relative fatness, tightness, and shortness of the string. The bassist must develop a sense of when to get off of this string and how to touch it to achieve the desired effect.

Fig. 9.2. Right-Hand Thumb Dampening Position for the Electric Bass

Physical Considerations

Right Hand

Many players anchor their right hand onto the instrument in one location via the thumb, when playing finger-style. Although this technique works well under most conditions, notes are occasionally left ringing, with no means of dampening them available. Allowing the location of the thumb to be movable solves this problem, as the thumb can act as a damper if it can roam across the strings.

The addition of the C and/or the B strings accentuates the dampening problem, demanding that the bassist have a movable location for the thumb (see fig. 9.2). The problems of over-ring (an open string vibrating out of sympathy to another) and strings left vibrating by rapid left-hand movement can best be solved by dampening with the thumb or its heel. Some dampening can also be accomplished by the left hand, but it must most often be free from this duty to do an effective job otherwise.

Players who double from 4- to 5- or 6-string instruments must be keenly aware of their physical playing habits. Many players are very habitual in their physical manner of playing and tend to mindlessly place their hands in familiar locations for non-musical reasons. Players of this type are in danger of the contraction of a severe case of wrongstringitis. Although wrongstringitis can affect either or both hands, it is most common in the right. Affected players will literally pluck the wrong strings due to a physical disorientation beyond their control. This disease can be fatal if it manifests itself under stressful circumstances, such as during an audition or an unaccompanied solo. To be cured, the player must eliminate this disorientation. Concentrated practice focusing on the right hand (or the left, if the affliction occurs there) and lots of switching back and forth between instruments is the general cure. Players with this malady should avoid the use of alcohol while performing.

Left Hand

The addition of strings to the electric bass physically widens the neck. This can cause problems for the left hand.

As is the case with right-hand problems associated with 5- and 6-string instruments, players who double are most at risk. Non-doubling players tend to avoid these problems through exact performance repetition from day to day; that is, by not switching back and forth to different ranged instruments, they avoid many of the problems. These problems are actually caused by the act of switching from a 4-string instrument to a 5- or a 6-string instrument without clear thought of what the switch entails.

A wider neck demands physical changes in the technique of the left hand, often setting up an environment of trouble. The changing of the angle of the left-hand wrist can cause strain on this joint and disorientation in the fingers. Strain manifests itself in pain and/or numbness; disorientation manifests itself in missed notes, wrongstringitis, or just going blank—yikes! In any case, the problem is generally caused by the player's difficulty in breaking overbearing 4-string habits. If the player switches instruments on a regular basis, this problem may tend to dissipate, but players who rely more on physical feel and positions rather than musical thought need to modify their performing technique through concentrated practice. The content of this practice should be physically focused on the problem area of the wrist and fingers, and mentally focused on clear musical thought. Clear musical thinking and reconditioning the physical parts used eventually overcomes these problems, allowing most players the pleasure of doubling at will with little extra effort.

CHAPTER 10

Creating and Maintaining an Effective Practice Schedule

To learn is to do. Let's pretend that you want to become a marathon runner. First, you would identify that you liked to run and seemed to be pretty adept at it. Eventually, you would need to hire a trainer with the knowledge of how to build your body properly. Next, you would need a coach to help you prepare for each individual race. You, your trainer, and your coach would all work in tandem to help you reach your goal. All the while, what would be your primary activity? Running, doing.

How long would this training, coaching, and doing go on? Well, this is the $64,000 question. Professional runners have coaches, trainers, and other hired help aiding them throughout their careers. Many casual runners seek professional help on a regular or an as-needed basis. No one in their right mind would attempt running a marathon without some guidance and rigorous training at a gym and in the field.

There are varying levels of preparation and varying levels of dependency on outside help needed to guide people to their goals. The keys are the setting of the goal and the doing, the action of going about attaining the goal. I call this doing *gyo* (a term I picked up from of an Eastern philosophy book, years ago). To me, gyo is conscious action, or doing, through guided force. It is taking the positive steps to gain through action. You might liken it to positive motivation. In so doing, it becomes easier to understand why some runners are so natural, such perennial winners, so all inspiring, so talented, so strong, so energetic, and so on. These runners possess gyo and know how to put it to good use. They have the knowledge of how to do.

And so it is, as a performer. But it is not as easy as I have made it seem to be. It is true that all you need do is set your goal and go about attaining it, but so much happens in between.

You teach yourself to read, you join a funk band, someone shows you how to slap, you get a show gig, you get a double bass for free from your uncle, you buy a bow, you take lessons, and then . . . you quit. Well, you get the point. We all have dynamic lives that cannot be predicted. So, how do we hold onto our goals?

The answer is simple. It is not so important to *hold on* to goals as it is to *have* goals. People change, goals change. What is important is gyo! You will need to reevaluate, and oftentimes change your goals. It is the gyo that causes this.

Think about all of your musician friends, for a minute. Let's put them into groups. Then you decide which group you fit into.

Beginners. Enough said. Beginners need to work on every aspect of their musicianship, and should have a well-rounded practice session, emphasizing technique, but also touching on ear training and musical development.

Street Players. These players are very adept at one or two styles, which they learned by ear from CDs or hanging with friends. They probably play casually a lot and might have a gig. Street players would be well-served to develop their reading skills and to explore styles beyond what they usually play.

Technically Challenged Players. They can't really play very well. Technically challenged players can't seem to get the feel or the technique down. They just don't understand what to do, but they love to play. Regular attention to technical studies, such as scales, arpeggios, and various fingerboard exercises, will help technically challenged players improve their skills, as will a good teacher.

Forcers. They read but sound like they are reading. When they play, you sometimes think you are listening to a machine. Practicing by ear, widening their use of articulations, and learning to improvise can help these players to develop a more human sound.

Jazzers. The jazzers possess natural talent. They can play almost anything that they hear and can fake their way through many situations, but they may be style restricted. Jazzers should broaden their abilities to include other styles into their repertoire.

Rockers. Rockers are limited jazzers. They are often stylistically restricted. Rockers should also work to bring other styles into their repertoire.

Semi-Pros. Semi-pros are conscientious players who take or took lessons and try to cover all the bases. Semi-pros are everywhere. They need only conscientious work and time to develop their abilities.

Pros. The pros seem to do it all with little or no effort and are paid well to do it. They are not necessarily prepared for any situation, but rather, are willing to prepare for any situation. Pros are committed to being the best and command respect from the rest. Their practice time can focus on learning more music and maintaining their chops.

Where do you fit in? Well, I have good news for you. You can fit in anywhere and still be successful. But it is important to see where you fit in. You must come to an understanding of where you are, if you are to have any chance at setting goals for your future.

Armed with self-knowledge, a love for music (and of course, for bass playing), and the desire to improve, you can set some goals.

You should spend a week or so initially thinking about what your goals might be. Jot down the ideas that come back again and again. Look over your ideas, think about your spot on the above list, consider your age, and consider your time constraints. Be honest with yourself, and evaluate your present state of motivation. All of this evaluating will gain you deeper self-knowledge and will point in positive directions. A goal or several goals will become clear in time. Then, you must commit to your goals.

It is at this point that the gyo takes over. After identifying goals, you must go about attaining them. We already know that this is through doing, but the doing must be directed. Unguided doing is chaos and can only lead to random results, at best.

As with the runner, the musician often seeks help from others more versed in the craft. Much knowledge and a clearer picture of oneself can be gained through a relationship with an instructor. I can't tell you how to find an instructor, but I can suggest some of the attributes that a qualified instructor will have.

Look for someone who exudes self-knowledge and confidence, someone playing all of the things that you want to play, someone able to communicate clearly. Find someone who is busy but can find time for you, someone who can motivate you, someone you can trust, someone with the patience of Job.

Use your teacher, trust your teacher, and if you must, fire your teacher. For many, the teacher/student relationship lasts a lifetime. Search until you find your teacher.

Your studies may require weekly lessons. Many teachers have the need to set up a regular schedule, and a regular schedule is usually the best regime for the student. Some prefer biweekly or monthly meetings.

Some sacrifices may need to be made to secure your lesson time. I was once on a waiting list for two years, hoping to study with Charlie Banacos, a noted music guru in the Boston area. When he finally called me with an opening, it was for 7:30 AM every Saturday! Needless to say, I made some major adjustments to be prepared for his guidance each Saturday morning.

In time, you may have lessons only as needed. This relationship will be malleable and ever-changing, but always guided by the teacher with the student's growth in mind.

So, you like playing the bass, you have done some soul searching, and you know where you are. You have taken the time to consider setting musical goals, and you have come to know that study, possibly through a teacher, will help you attain your goal. It's about time you learned how to practice.

You know what they say, "practice makes perfect." I don't know if it's true or not, but it sure can help.

Consider how valuable your time is, and realize that you will be investing your time into your practice. Don't waste your time, value it. When you realize that your practice time is a major means of attaining your goals, it becomes clear how important this time is. Your practice time must be planned, dynamic, and regular to be most effective. Haphazard practice does achieve results, but never of the magnitude attainable through the rigors and discipline of regular, intense practice.

The specific content and duration of your practice will be determined by your individual circumstances. Your teacher can be a great aid in determining these factors. There are some general guidelines that will help you create and maintain a good practice schedule.

Humans are creatures of habit, living in a world that repeats itself every day. With this said, the most important aspect about your practice schedule is that it needs to be regular—preferably, daily. You will achieve the best results if you can integrate your practice schedule into your daily life. In so doing, you can actually cause yourself to "need to practice," which is a great help for those of us without optimum motivation. One could go further and consider practicing every day at the same time. For some, this is the optimum, but others need be careful of burnout or getting into a rut. Self-knowledge and a sense of human nature are the keys to getting yourself on track to a successful practice schedule.

Always consider your ultimate goal, but now, be ready to set interim, short-term goals that will ultimately lead you to your final goal. Reevaluate every six months or so to be sure you are still on track or to decide whether you need to adjust or change your track.

To help create a "need to practice," start off by not allowing yourself enough time to accomplish all of your tasks. Stay focused and work hard. Don't waste time. You will realize that you need more time to finish your work. After a short while, you should add time, as needed. Never alter your practice habits drastically, all at once, as this will cause chaos within your musical anatomy.

I have heard of players utilizing practice times from ten minutes to ten hours per day, achieving success at each end of the scale. Of course, success is also a relative term. One practicing ten minutes a day cannot expect to make great leaps in their abilities from week to week. On the other hand, one practicing ten hours a day may need to get a life. Or maybe, they have found one.

Performing regularly on gigs, or just playing in a garage band, can restrict the amount of your practice time. For most players, the exertion of "real" playing far surpasses the strains attained in the practice room. Performers with day gigs that tax the muscles of their musical anatomy, or players participating in sporting events that use these muscles, need to be mindful of their bodies' physical limits. They may also need to restrict their practice time.

A practice routine is an exercise program with academic material incorporated into it. As such, I again recommend that the player seek out a competent instructor with whom to work out the physical and mental dilemmas related to playing bass. The specific choices of exercises and the incorporation of academic material can be individualized by the performer (student) and the teacher. There are, however, three areas that practice material can be classified. All are equally necessary for successful practice.

1. **Maintain and Build.** Each player comes into this with certain physical and mental ability. As long as we have proper physical technique and our academic foundation is not flawed, we must first maintain our current level, and in time, we need to build upon it. Specific fingering exercises, scale and arpeggio patterns, and stamina exercises are often used for this purpose. Occasionally playing or reading pieces previously mastered can also help to fulfill this area of practice.

2. **Personal Interests and Needs.** All players have tunes that they want to learn. Many of these can be quite difficult to learn and play. This type of material needs to be incorporated into the practice schedule. Learning can be accomplished through reading or transcribing. In learning a piece from a CD, take the time to transcribe the music on paper first. This action will help you learn the piece more quickly, help to locate errors, and help to improve your reading ability.

You don't always love what you have to play, but since you love playing bass, you play whatever you need to play. Many players feel this way, and so, there arises a need to incorporate material that you love into your practice time. Choose material that has personal meaning to you. This type of practice can be particularly enjoyable.

3. **Survival Skills.** There are sometimes things that must be learned in order to survive. You are playing a show next week, and the part is too difficult for you to sight-read. You just joined a band, your first gig is this Saturday, and you need to learn eighteen tunes from a tape. You have an audition with an orchestra next week, and they are going to have you play excerpts from Beethoven's Fifth Symphony. These are all examples of needs for your immediate survival as a bass player. Not only does this material need to be incorporated into your practice schedule; at times, this material will supersede all other.

In the end, it is a blend of these that you should strive for, leaning, at times, in one direction or the other, depending on which direction the wind blows.

No matter how long your session is, you need to incorporate four or five specific sections to your practice schedule. If you allow an hour, you could allot about ten to fifteen minutes to each area. As you increase your overall practice time, the centerpieces need to be greatly lengthened while the periphery material may increase only slightly.

Most practice should start with stretching. It is not good to play or stretch, seriously, when cold. If you are cold, play lightly to bring your muscles up to a warmer, more comfortable temperature. When your fingers are at a comfortable temperature, you are ready to begin your stretching. This initial stretching is not meant to be serious, drawn-out stretching, but is intended to loosen up and prepare your musical anatomy for what is to come. All of the areas used during performance should be stretched before any serious practicing is attempted. Many players have "weak spots" or problem areas that they may give some special attention to. Many players don't feel the need to stretch. If they are lucky enough to still be performing in twenty years, they will have changed their minds, and in fact, may need the stretch more than the rest of us, after not stretching for twenty years. Refer to fig. 12.3 for some useful stretches.

After a moderate stretching period, time should be devoted to warming up. Your muscles need to warm up further to function at optimum. This is especially true in colder climates. Find some slow, easy material to use. Repetitive material that uses all of the fingers equally and works all of the arm, shoulder, and back muscles to some degree is good. Some players like to work in some sight-reading at this point.

These two areas of stretching and warming up can be mixed or reversed to some degree as your physical needs and temperatures dictate. If you are a particularly cold-blooded person, or during winter months, it is best to warm up some and then stretch, possibly completing the warm-up after stretching. Muscles do not properly stretch if cold, and stretching cold muscles can cause injury. Stretching should never be painful. If it is, you are going too far.

The first centerpiece of your practice regime should be *skills* practice—the scales, arpeggios, melodic patterns, chord progressions, and the like, that constitute the foundation of our bass playing. Much of this material will be suggested by your teacher. This practice needs to be intense and ever improving. Additions and subtractions to the materials should be made from time to time. This is mental as well as physical practice, and for most players, it is quite dynamic and fluid.

As your practice time increases, and especially if you are not playing gigs on a regular basis, you should incorporate the second centerpiece: gig situation playing. You must put yourself in the mind of a performer on a gig and play on. This must be as intense as the gigs you can imagine. Concentration is the key to this type of practice, as you could play an entire set of jazz standards or a Mahler symphony from start to finish. No stopping is allowed. Treat this like the real thing. If you have the time for more than one set, take a break and do it again. Gig situation playing is also both mental and physical. It is intended to build physical stamina and concentration.

When your time is becoming short, go to the cool down. It is just the opposite of the warm-up. Relax a little, play something simple, let your mind begin to wander. This can also be a good time to bring yourself back to Earth mentally, and practice a little reading.

Just before you are finished, stretch again. This stretching should be more strenuous than before, since your muscles will be quite warm. Your muscles will stretch quite easily. Hold your stretches for about thirty seconds, if possible. You will find your flexibility will improve from this stretching, and the possibility of injury will decrease. Stretching should never be painful.

Practice is hard work. It consists of physical exertion and guided thinking. It must be this way if you want it to work for you. On the other hand, you may have occasionally experienced wonderful personal performances when you seemingly had no thoughts. This is the balance of the world of opposites in action. There exists thought and no thought. Neither can exist without the other, and each is dependent upon the other. Our ultimate objective is to exercise thought during practice and no thought during performance. This is a difficult ideal to obtain, but the knowledge of its existence helps us to achieve it.

Now, all you have to do is fill in the blanks for your own practice schedule. To keep yourself in top shape, I also recommend regular non-musical exercise. I'm talking about swimming, running, playing soccer, going to the gym, biking—you get the idea. Bass playing doesn't do a lot for the physical health of our hearts. In fact, the bars, clubs, practice rooms, and restaurants we find ourselves in can actually cause damage to our hearts, and there is nothing worse than a bass player with a damaged heart. Consider getting yourself into some regular activities that promote the well being of your heart. Join a soccer team, buy a bike, or my best idea, join the YMCA or another full service gym.

CHAPTER 11
Warm-Ups

All bassists need to develop an approach to warming up, or preparing their performance anatomy for action. Casual players may not see the need to warm up, due to the fact that they may not presently be taxing their muscles. But as they age, or as performance opportunities become more intense, physical warm-up will become a necessity. Professional players must be at the top of their game at all times, and a methodical warm-up is generally the manner in which they begin a performance or practice. This need to warm up has the added advantage of forcing you to get to the gig early, helping you avoid being docked or fired, as many latecomers are.

Warm-up exercises should have a purpose, or two. Warm-ups need not be difficult; in fact, they should be simple in nature and should not cause stress. Speed is not a factor. Most warm-ups are best performed at slow to medium tempi. Effective warm-up exercises use all of your physical performance anatomy in relatively equal amounts, preparing all parts to function efficiently in performance. Players need to design warm-up programs that suit their performance requirements. Warm-up programs may differ from day to day, depending on the player's immediate needs. There are a number of benefits to be gained from proper warming up.

Personal Preparation

Your muscles function best at around 103 degrees. You may have a gig in Hartford on February 10. After dragging all of your gear into the club, setting up, and pulling out your bass, you might notice that your fingers are still cold, real cold. Might I suggest a little warming up before the first set? This may be an extreme case, but even muscles that are just slightly chilled can be seriously injured by strenuous work. Don't forget that your fingers are an extremity on your body, and as such, are cooler than your central body. It is a good idea to lightly warm up even on a warm day. Remember that your body temperature is below the 103 degrees that your muscles like for performance, so the warm-up prepares your muscles for the work to come.

The warm-up needs to establish good blood circulation, warm the muscles, and warm the flesh so that the sense of touch feels comfortable. Once all of these needs are met, you are ready to perform.

Effective warm-ups can also prepare the performer mentally for the performance that is about to ensue. Try to make your warm-up mentally stimulating so that your mind can begin to focus on your musical task at hand. Playing all of the major scales, focusing on articulations and fingerings, is a good example of a warm-up that will attend to the needs of all of your fingers equally. Your hands, arms, back, and musical brain will also warm up with an exercise like this.

Technical Promotion

I do not recommend reading warm-up exercises. In fact, I discourage it. It is best to observe *yourself* as you warm up, not the written page. This self-observation can be accomplished visually or mentally. In either case, the warm-up time affords an opportunity to observe our own technique and make corrections or alterations as we see fit.

The slow, direct nature of warm-up exercises makes them excellent devices to strengthen or change one's performance technique. Body angles can be carefully monitored and adjusted, yielding effects immediately. Posture modifications can be attempted and results can be readily observed. In short, we can observe ourselves and take immediate action on what we observe that improves our personal performance technique. Since warm-ups are similar from day to day, regular technical comparisons can be made.

Strengthening Weaknesses

All of us perceive weaknesses within ourselves, and oftentimes, these weaknesses are physical. Maybe you have a weak third finger on your left hand or problems with your right-hand thumb becoming too tense. Problems such as these can be initially addressed during your warm-up.

It is not good to create stress during a warm-up. You should never fatigue any particular muscle as you just begin to play. But you can design some of your warm-up exercises to pay just a little more attention to your weak spots. Not only can the extra physical activity be advantageous, but awareness of your weaknesses will aid in your gaining strength in these areas.

You may have a left-hand exercise that you perform that repeats finger patterns of 1 2 3 4 over and over in various locations on the neck. Focusing on the 3 each time and placing a mental accent on it will strengthen this move without adding stress to your exercise. If your right-hand thumb is tight or sore, play a one-string open roll at medium intensity, and concentrate solely on the thumb, forcing it to remain relaxed.

You are attempting to isolate certain parts mentally, but continue on as usual, physically exercising all parts equally. As you achieve success with this method, you may go one step further, and begin to isolate these areas physically, being careful never to stress the area being built up. After all, this is still the warm-up portion of your performance. Now, your left-hand exercise might be modified to 1 3 2 3 4, or 1 2 3 4 3, your right-hand exercise may increase in tempo, or you may shift your concentration to the thumb muscle, actually tightening and loosening repeatedly as you continue to play the open-string roll.

Reup

I mentioned earlier that players need to develop warm-up programs to fit their own performance needs. Performers go through many stages of physical condition during their careers, each stage presenting different physical demands. One particular stage that all bassists encounter at some point is the need to get back in good playing form after a layoff. The bass is a particularly physically demanding instrument. After a layoff period, it is not usually possible to just start playing at full steam without some serious physical discomfort.

This preparation to perform in top form after a layoff I call the *reup*. The reup is completely physical in nature. The performer has no need to enhance his musical abilities, but is only interested in rebuilding muscles and calluses so as to allow for painless performances.

This is the time for serious warm-ups. Remember that warm-ups use all of the performance anatomy relatively equally, and the rested bass player will need all parts rebuilt. Perform warm-up type exercises until your fingertips are slightly tender; do not develop blisters. Try to repeat warm-ups as often as possible daily, increasing intensity as physical form returns. Practice in this manner is not actually warming up, but rather, borrowing material from your warm-up programs to recondition your physical performance anatomy.

One is often required to perform immediately after a layoff period. This can be a very dangerous situation. Blisters, muscle strain, or worse can put you out of commission for a long time, so use careful judgment concerning hard playing after a layoff.

I have created for myself a dummy 12-inch practice neck from an old double bass neck someone was throwing away. I attached a tuner at one end and drilled a hole at the other to run a string through. I use a screw for a nut. The string can be tightened and crudely raised and lowered by means of a movable bridge (a piece of small pipe). I call this device my "callus preserver." When I must travel without my bass, I just carry it along and squeeze it as necessary. It doesn't take up any space and works great on long airplane trips. At times, I carry this in my car and I can actually warm up on the way to the gig. This is not a very rewarding activity, musically, but I can avoid all of the reup hassles noted above. Maybe you can think of a creative way to solve your future reup problems.

Good Habit Cultivation

We are all creatures of habit. We all thrive on regularity. This is human nature tuning to the regularity of the universe. By addressing your instrument in a similar manner each time you play, you are setting up a series of habits—good habits. The playing of the warm-up exercise sets up your mind to begin functioning in a musical fashion. The muscles are prepared to react in a predictable manner due to the repetition of this process on a regular basis. You warm up, you play, you enjoy, you learn, and so on. You cultivate a need to warm up by warming up; this need to warm up causes you to warm up the next time that you play, which improves your performance ability and mentality each time you play. This can become an endless stream of positive actions perpetuated by your own desire to improve. This same line of thinking can be carried over to all of your practice efforts.

Warm-Up Exercises

Double

Transpose to all strings, first bowing as shown above the staff and then as shown below. There are many creative ways to extend this exercise.

1. Transpose to all strings.

2. Transpose to all strings.

Electric

1. Transpose to all strings.

2. Transpose to all strings. Continue up each string to the octave or beyond. Be sure to play back to the starting note.

Fig. 11.1. Warm-Up Exercises

CHAPTER 12
A Lifetime of Healthy Performance

During my musical career, I have experienced a number of physical problems that have caused me considerable concern for my performance health. I have had numerous personal and professional consultations with orthopedic and neurological specialists. So, I speak from my experiences as a performer, an educator, and one who is concerned about physical health, not as a medical expert. It is my intention to set forth some general information related to this subject so as to help the reader become more aware of its importance, and possibly to inspire action towards conducting further related research. If you are experiencing any physical problems, such as those I will discuss in this chapter, I cannot stress enough the need to establish a relationship with a qualified physician whose expertise lies in the area of your particular problem.

Most major cities with a sizable population of performing artists (dancers, musicians, etc.) have clinics or doctors that specialize in performing arts medicine. Since this can be a very narrow field, the doctors often must be found through their affiliation with a major hospital. Make every attempt to seek out these specialists, if the need arises, for they are well-equipped to understand the physical ailments related to bass playing. If you cannot find an arts doctor, the field of sports medicine is closely related. After all, playing the bass is a lot like being a baseball catcher.

I have included a brief list of medical definitions that might be useful to the bass player, at the end of this chapter. For more detailed information, please consult with a doctor or an appropriate medical text.

Performance Anatomy

Most bass players consider their hands and fingers as the most important parts of their bodies. Although it is true that these are the body parts that actually touch the instrument and finish the task of producing music, the overall act of playing the bass is reliant upon the entire performance anatomy.

The governing part of your performance anatomy is your brain. It must already contain any ideas that you intend to act upon during a performance. Quality music is rarely an accident, but rather, is the result of long hours of thoughtful practice and preparation.

The brain differs from the rest of the performance anatomy in that it alone generates action through thought. It is not a muscle, but it is the control center for the muscles. It is important to keep the brain well-nourished and filled with the ideas of music. Stress and other factors that occupy your attention affect your ability to produce quality music.

If you perform standing, your performance anatomy gains support starting at the toes and progressing through the feet, up the legs, through the lower back, and culminating in the upper back. For those players who sit while performing, support begins in the pelvis and progresses through the lower back to the upper back. These structures may not be directly involved in the production of music, but their support is necessary for the ultimate product to be comfortably produced.

The actual musical thoughts produced in the brain are sent as commands via nerves through the neck and upper back area, under the shoulder and past the elbow, through the wrist and hand to the fingers. The pathway for this signal must be clear. It needs to be healthy and unobstructed.

So, in a nanosecond, your body and head are supported by your legs and back, your brain conceives of musical action, and your fingers react, guided by the angles created at your shoulders, elbows, and wrists. I hope you can begin to see how complicated this bass playing business can be.

There really are no parts of the body that don't get involved in the bass player's actions. Overall good physical and mental health and well-being will allow most bassists to prosper through a lifelong career.

General Factors to Consider

There are a number of general factors affecting a bassist's ability to obtain and maintain good physical performance technique. Some or all of these factors may affect you at any given time in your career. Many are avoidable, some are unavoidable. Proper attention to them can eliminate small physical annoyances that may grow into career-stopping ailments. Paying attention to these general factors can extend your performance career well past retirement age.

The most inevitable factor for all of us to consider is age, or growing older. If we are lucky, it will happen to all of us, gracefully. But it won't happen by accident. You must consider how your muscles feel and react as you age. Consider how your spine will feel after having a Jazz Bass hanging on it for twenty-five years or so. Listen to your body as it ages, and be vigilant about your health. If you enjoy performing, talk to some elderly bass players. Listen to their concerns; you may be hearing yourself, one day.

Many people are born with structural inadequacies or abnormalities. These can be skeletal or muscular in nature. An abnormality could be as major as having webbed fingers or as minor as having a slightly misshaped metacarpal bone. Some structural abnormalities can be corrected, but most require lifelong special attention and technique-related adjustments. Physical abnormalities can limit the amount of time a performer is able to perform, so it becomes very important that you use all your practice time wisely.

Your day-to-day lifestyle can prolong or shorten your career, depending on your living preferences. In general, good habits are as easy to form as bad habits. You merely must convince yourself of the positive effects that are caused by good habits.

Some of our bad habits have a direct impact on our performance anatomy. The excessive use of alcohol, tobacco, and salt can cause vitamin deficiency throughout the body. Caffeine and nicotine may constrict the blood vessels, lessening blood flow to areas in need of nourishment, and raising blood pressure. If you do use these products, try to exercise moderation. Always walk the middle path.

Nowadays, it seems as though everyone has a bottle of water with them. It looks so yuppyish, but consuming plenty of water each day is one of the best things you can do to maintain good health. Don't be embarrassed to carry that plastic bottle around with you on gigs or to the practice room.

Musicians who play at night and have a day gig often neglect obtaining the proper amount of rest and sleep. Rest and sleep are needed to allow the physical components of your body to regenerate. The proper amount of sleep is also necessary for good mental health. Many musicians who must work days and nights look for short power naps during the day for supplemental rest. This can begin by just resting for 15 minutes or so at a similar time each day. In time, you will be relaxed enough to fall asleep for 10 minutes or so. This type of rest cannot replace quality sleep, but for many, it can help to lessen fatigue over several very busy days.

Proper diet is also necessary for good physical and mental health, and it aids in gaining quality sleep time. Everybody knows how much easier it is to play the bass after three portions of fruits and veggies. Try to avoid that late night dinner after a gig. Eating before sleep lessens the quality of sleep.

Probably the single best thing you can do for yourself is to get good regular exercise. Not only will this keep your muscles in great shape, but it will increase your metabolism and strengthen your heart. As bass players, we get some great exercise loading equipment and performing, but we rarely get out of breath, which is necessary for good cardiovascular development. Take some time to swim, bike, run, or box. Do some aerobics with a friend, or join a class. Try some strength training to avoid physical problems in your future. A half hour to an hour of good exercise three times a week is all you need to stay in good shape. Exercise your large muscle groups the most. You may actually need to avoid exercise of your hands and forearms, if you are performing every day, so as to avoid overuse. Your exercise program should include stretching. I illustrate some stretches that are particularly useful to bass players later in this chapter. There are a number of books available on exercise and health, some of which I have listed in the Resources section at the end of this book.

Your technique, or the physical manner in which you play, may have a great effect on the longevity of your performing career. Poor technique will overtax your muscles and bones, causing undue strain that may lead to temporary or permanent injuries. Since we people come in all sizes, technique variations are commonplace. A respected teacher or a reputable performer can help you with technique-related issues.

Occasionally, you will find a musician who eats, breathes, and sleeps music, but most of us need non-musical diversions. By being involved in non-musical activities, we avoid becoming jaded to music, and we can keep our musical thoughts fresh and spontaneous. A non-musical diversion is any activity that takes us totally away from our musical life. Going to the gym, surfing the Web, working on old trucks, collecting coins, and going out dancing are all examples of non-musical diversions. Sometimes, we must try very hard to keep music out of our minds while we are on our diversions, but with a little practice, we can all get away to renew ourselves.

And, of course, since we are now in the twenty-first century, we all know how important it is to have a positive outlook toward life. It is true that life is so much easier with a positive attitude. We must all work at centering on the enjoyment we derive from our music, and take joy in the work necessary to attain our goals. Try to look forward to positive experiences while correcting your faults. Attitude makes all the difference.

Factors for Special Consideration

A number of circumstances heighten the possibility of performance-related injury. All of us experience a number of these circumstances during our playing careers. This fact alone does not mean that we will have physical problems resulting from our experience. But these special situations heighten our chances for subsequent physical problems. The more these factors occur at one time, the greater the risk of physical injury.

Improper posture or the lack of adequate performance conditioning can cause many stress-related physical problems. These problems can be avoided by regular practice and proper technique. Good physical conditioning requires regular and prolonged effort.

Changing instruments requires you to use your muscles in slightly different ways, causing body angles to change to some degree. Typically, the muscles and tissues at strained points are built up through regular systematic practice. Suddenly adjusting the locations of these stress points can cause injury. If a new instrument causes you to make technical adjustments, allow ample time for your body to react. Players who double on several different basses are not as susceptible to this problem, as their bodies gradually become properly callused and are used to the adjustments necessary.

Probably the most common cause of performance related injuries to bass players is a sudden increase in playing time or drastic fluctuations of time spent playing from day to day. Our body works best under regular conditions. Suddenly adding large amounts of performance time can have career-stopping consequences. It is always best to increase performance intervals gradually. One must be foresighted and prepare properly for physical activities in the future.

Suddenly changing your technique, be it a good change or a bad change, can be an invitation for an injury. Here again, you must remember that your body tends to get used to what it has been doing. When you suddenly change activities, especially drastically, you are demanding new actions from muscles that have been trained to react in your old, familiar manner. Take the time that is necessary to make drastic technical changes gradually.

Many bass players have other jobs. Indeed, I have already mentioned that it is good to have non-musical diversions. Care must be taken, however, when a non-musical activity uses the same muscles as your bass playing. A job that requires typing and mousing on a computer all day does not mesh well with an evening of bass playing. Similarly, shucking oysters at a seafood bar is not a good complement to bass playing on the side. The smaller muscles of the hands and fingers are especially at risk, but a bassist could injure his shoulder if he swims too many miles in a week. Listen to your body when it cries out.

Some people just don't know when to stop. You may know someone who claims to practice ten hours a day and plays gigs too. Well, if he is telling the truth, it is my hope that he has conditioned himself very well. Even if he has, he is a candidate for muscle and connecting tissue misuse and overuse. There is only so much that can be required of our tissue structures before they need to rest and rejuvenate. Even with perfect conditioning, much rest and rejuvenation is necessary. A certain type of mentality tends to deny this fact, opening the player up to a host of physical maladies.

Cold can be a wonderful aid in healing, but it is detrimental to the working muscle. Muscles perform at their peak at around 103 degrees. This is why we warm up. This is why we avoid performing in the snow. Certainly, light playing while chilled will not be a problem for most players, but aggressive playing, with cold muscles, is an invitation for a serious injury. Cold muscles do not possess the ability to be as accurate as warm muscles do, also casting a shadow on your performance ability while chilled.

Many players incorporate excessive, unnecessary movement into their playing technique. Although extraneous movement does not, in itself, affect your musical output, it brings on early fatigue. Performing while harboring physical or mental tension also brings on early fatigue. Many players are forced to perform regularly in a fatigued state due to hectic living schedules. This is quite unhealthy. Generally, aside from inviting physical injury, this type of activity produces a less than acceptable musical result.

I'm sure you all know a macho guy who can just work right through any pain. He seems to be able to literally master the pain. In sports, this is called the "good sport's attitude." In bass playing, we call it "stupid." Listen to your body, and react to what it is telling you. When you feel unusual pains that don't go away, stop playing and find some help. Denial is a very strong force, acting within all of us at one time or another, but consider that denial may cost you all of your future performances.

These factors listed above can be controlled with some common-sense effort on your part, but there are a number of special factors over which you do not have complete control.

A previous injury, such as a broken bone or deep slice to the hand, can create an inherent weak spot that will need your constant attention if you are to perform pain-free. Previous injuries often cause one to make adjustments to common performance technique.

Having a virus or other current infection, be it chronic or otherwise, should curtail your performance activities. Viruses and other infections, in general, have a negative effect on your entire body, causing it to be in a weakened state. In this weakened state, you are more vulnerable to injury through normal or slightly overactive playing. Metabolic and endocrine problems will also affect the ability of the body to rest, heal, rejuvenate, and ward off injury. These problems require special care and a trip to the doctor. Don't just keep working; you might make the whole band sick.

We have no control over our genetics, but genetics can play a major role in your performance career. All your physical attributes came from your ancestors, and many of your physical shortcomings came from the same place. If you have a family history of certain ailments, you may be more likely to develop the same kinds of problems. Knowledge of your family's medical history can be an aid in avoiding many performance injuries. Get to know your grandparents.

The more of these circumstances you encounter, the more at risk you may be for a performance injury. If you broke your finger last summer, just bought a new bass, just picked up a day gig as a massage therapist, have a slipped disc, and figure that you can work through all this pain no problem, you might be in big trouble.

Common Bass Player Ailments

As of this writing, I have played bass for thirty-four years and taught bass for twenty-seven. My expertise is in performance and education. Consequently, it is not my intention to play doctor, but I would like to outline some of the most common bass player ailments that I have observed as an educator/performer. Although many conditions can be corrected through performance technique adjustments and supervised rehabilitation, there always seems to be another bass player waiting in the wings, ready to fall victim to one or more of these maladies. Most of these ailments can generally be classified under the heading of *repetitive motion disorders*. They occur because we perform the same motions over and over, beyond our physical limits. All of these disorders can be affected by the general and special consideration factors listed above. Many bass players attempt to manage these disorders by the use of over-the-counter drugs, such as aspirin, naproxen sodium, ibuprofen, and acetaminophen. It may be all right to manage an occasional twitch in this manner, but it is foolish to self-diagnose and prescribe your own medicine when a serious problem may be present. Seek out a doctor when your body asks you to.

Tendinitis

During normal use, the tendon gently slides back and forth in a lubricated sheath as body movements occur. When movements become reckless, prolonged, or when an external injury has been incurred by the tendon or sheath, pain is generated and tendinitis occurs. Mild tendinitis may heal in a week, with proper treatment. Severe tendinitis can last for months and may bring a promising career to a grinding halt.

Tendinitis can occur at any location where bone and muscle join. For the bassist, the most common locations are the thumbs, the hands, the elbows, and shoulders. Symptoms include severe pain, limited motion at the location of the injury, and redness or inflammation in the area.

Most cases of tendinitis can be cured with proper medical attention, but repeated injury to the same area, or not allowing an injury to completely heal, can create a chronic problem.

Tendinitis is the most common ailment experienced by bass players. It can affect any and all of the joints between your head and your fingers. Your best defense is proper conditioning and good technique.

Bursitis

The *bursa* provides lubrication at joints. This lubrication is provided for all the parts that join at a joint, including bones and tendons. If the bursa becomes irritated for any reason, pain occurs in the affected joint. The elbow and the shoulder are the most common locations of bursitis in bass players.

It is widely believed that genetics plays a role in selecting candidates for bursitis attacks. Other causes include poor conditioning and injury to the bursa.

Bursitis can be quite painful, and it is really not possible to perform if you are experiencing a severe case. It would not be wise either, as continued irritation to the bursa will prolong the rehabilitation time. Swelling and inflammation are often present alongside the acute pain.

Don't be thinking that bursitis is just for old guys. Young bass players mistreat their bodies too, and although bursitis is more common in older players, it can strike teens as well.

Bursitis can be a complicated disorder to treat. Doctors generally recommend ice, heat, elevation, rest, surgery, medication—you get the picture. As is the case with tendinitis, your best defense is proper preparation and sensible playing.

Nerve Compression

The nerves that operate your hands and fingers originate in the brain. On the way to the fingers, they pass through the shoulder, the elbow, and the wrist. At these locations, there is a danger of entrapping or pinching. There are a number of specific nerve entrapment disorders, including the most famous, carpal tunnel syndrome. Nerve compressions can be painful and are usually accompanied by numbness. The location of the numbness helps your doctor determine which nerve is being entrapped and where.

Flexing or stretching can often cause a nerve compression to hurt more, making proper performance technique impossible. Solutions to nerve-related problems always include plenty of rest from playing. Serious nerve impingements left untreated can cause permanent damage, as nerves eventually die due to the lack of nourishment. It is important to identify the source and cause of any nerve-related problem and to begin problem solving at once. The healing time required by injured nerves is quite long, so be patient with yourself.

Ganglion Cyst

Ganglions are calcium deposits. They can range from small and insignificant to large and very painful. The most common locations that warrant attention by bassists are above or below the wrist and above or below the hand. Ganglions are usually hard, and can range in size from minuscule to marble size, as they form gradually over long periods of time. Formation is usually relative to a tendon and is often caused by a previous injury to the cyst location, or a defect in the tendon sheath that allows fluid to leak, subsequently hardening into the cyst.

Ganglions may dissipate by themselves, if given proper treatment. If the injury is not tended to, the ganglion may continue to grow and require surgical removal. It is possible to have a large ganglion and not experience pain and discomfort, but if formation is related to bass playing, the cyst most often causes varying degrees of discomfort, often requiring removal.

You can reduce the risk of a ganglion developing by taking extra care to protect your hands from trauma and taking the time to warm up and stretch before performances.

Muscle Strain

Muscle strain is caused by overusing or misusing muscles. Misuse could be related to not getting enough rest and sleep or poor nutrition. Rest and good health practices correct this problem.

The pain associated with muscle strain is located in the muscles. Therefore, it is not usually located at the joints. The most common muscle strain for bassists is in the left top forearm.

Muscle strain can often be a forerunner of other problems. It can be an initial indication of the eventual wear of bad habits. It is therefore important to step back and evaluate your performance and lifestyle habits when muscle strain and pain are present.

Focal Dystonia and Chronic Muscle Pain Syndrome

Focal dystonia and chronic muscle pain syndrome are often confused with each other, but they are different.

Focal dystonia is thought to be caused by excessive repetitive practice. It does not usually present pain, but rather, involves the loss of coordination of specific muscles. It usually starts as only occurring while at the instrument, but gradually incorporates itself into daily life activities. It is rarely experienced by casual performers and is very unusual, but more common, for the professional. Successful treatment is possible but not assured.

Chronic muscle pain syndrome, as its name suggests, involves pain. This pain is not usually severe, but rather is often generalized as overall fatigue or general soreness and stiffness. Oftentimes, the soreness extends throughout the body, being more severe in the areas of performance usage. Treatment often includes massage therapy, rest, and cold packs.

These two conditions are not common, but it is possible for professional performers to develop problems that may include them. Knowing your own body and how it functions, along with healthy performance habits, will generally shield you from these disorders.

Back Problems

We hang basses on our backs, we crouch over our instruments, we schlep heavy, bulky equipment around on a daily basis—it's no wonder so many bass players have back problems. It is obvious that people in our profession can develop problems with their backs, and there are numerous conditions that can develop. Common problems include muscle strains or tears, nerve pinches, and damaged disks. There are also a number of congenital problems that can afflict our backs. Any back-related problem is serious, and all require professional help. Never lose sight of the importance of back support. Doctors, massage therapists, and chiropractors can all be of help in solving your problems.

But it is best to avoid problems initially. Practice good posture. Keep your back fit through regular cardiovascular exercise and weight training. Eat nutritious foods, and make every effort to keep your weight close to ideal. Get the proper amount of rest and sleep, paying attention to good sleeping positions and what you are sleeping on. Lift with your knees, keeping your back straight. Seek professional help with your performance posture from successful performers.

Blisters

Blisters may form on fingertips and around the thumb. You are particularly susceptible to them when you suddenly play a great deal after a layoff period, increase your normal playing time drastically, raise the action of your instrument, play much harder than usual, or change your technique to expose soft skin to string wear.

A blister is a temporary inconvenience that will heal in time, but it will cause much discomfort in the interim. It is not wise to continue to play after a blister begins to develop, but sometimes this is necessary as demanded by your job. Blisters will almost always eventually split open and peel, causing you to lose what protection you may have built up.

Smart players avoid blisters through preparation. Experienced players are able to sense the amount of callus necessary to make playing comfortable, and they see to maintaining the calluses necessary for their current performance needs. After a layoff, callus preparation is necessary in advance of performance dates, or blisters may develop.

Controlling blisters comes with experienced playing. Most professional players maintain their calluses even through a layoff. Most bass players feel naked without their calluses.

RICE and Rehabilitation

RICE stands for rest, ice, compression, and elevation. RICE is the universal cure for acute injuries. Rest the injury, apply cold, compress the injury if open, and elevate to control blood flow.

For the performance-related injuries that bass players experience, the aspects of rest and ice are most useful. All of the injuries listed above require rest for the healing process to begin. Ice, or cold, is used as a means to calm down inflammation without the use of drugs. The use of ice also brings the area treated to a restful state quickly, further hastening the healing process.

Ice should be combined with rest, for if ice is used and work follows, major injury is more likely. Muscles work best when warmed up. The same can be said of other tissues used during performance. If a player with thumb tendinitis ices his hand and then goes about playing, he is risking deeper, more complicated injury and defeating the healing process.

Rehabilitation can begin as soon as an injury is properly diagnosed.

The first step of rehabilitation is eliminating the injury. This is where your doctor's guidance is most useful. Always follow your doctor's advice in healing your injury. Take as much time as is needed to complete the job.

Once healing has been achieved and pain is no longer present, you must begin to restore proper movement. This initially involves simple, non-stressful movements designed to lay the groundwork for proper performance technique.

When your biomechanics are restored and you can perform the proper movements without pain, you will need to incorporate stretching. This will begin the restoration of the flexibility needed to perform properly.

If all goes well, the next step is to begin to build strength. Strength is best built through progressive exercises that are sport specific. This means that it is time to play the bass again. Begin slowly, and pay careful attention to proper technique. Some injuries may require technical adjustments. These adjustments can begin to be accomplished at this stage.

The final stage of rehabilitation is building endurance. This step is merely an extension of the previous step. Practice should involve conditioning exercises and much repetition. Most of this work will again be sport specific, at the bass. Care must continue to be taken to adhere to proper technique, and performance time must be increased gradually. Never hurry.

Preventive Care and Maintenance

It is always better to avoid an injury in the first place and avoid rehabilitation altogether. There are a number of simple things that, if given proper consideration, can greatly reduce your chances of injury.

Pay careful attention to your body posture. Observe your stress points while standing and performing. Look for ways to reduce this stress. Double-bass players might consider using a stool, but be careful to maintain good posture and biomechanics while on the stool. Generally, the stool should not reduce your height by more than a couple of inches.

If you play electric, check out your strap. Generally, wider is better, as weight is more evenly distributed with a wide strap.

Use a mirror when you practice. It is sometimes easier to see discomfort in early stages than it is to feel it. Playing should be fun, and it should feel good. It should look comfortable too. Avoid sharp angles, a slumping body, standing on one foot, and holding the bass too low or too high.

Pay particular attention to your hand/arm posture. Try to round out sharp angles into circles (see fig. 12.1). Sharp angles encourage stress. Consider the strength of a circle. Consider the strength of your hand holding a large orange. Now consider how much weaker is your grip of a golf ball held by the fingertips (see fig. 12.2). Try to emulate the more powerful position at the instrument.

Fig. 12.1. Hand/Arm Posture

Keep yourself in good physical condition through regular exercise that is not related to bass playing. You can't expect your arms and hands to function well if you neglect the rest of your body.

Stretching is an often-overlooked aspect of practice, conditioning, and maintaining good physical health. Stretching should never be done when cold. Moderate stretching can be beneficial after a modest warm-up, and more intense stretching can be accomplished after practice or performance. Stretching should not hurt. I recommend avoiding the use of stationary objects to aid in your stretching. Stretches should be held for about twenty seconds or so to be beneficial (see fig. 12.3). For more detailed information on stretching, I recommend consulting a physical therapist or checking out your dog or cat.

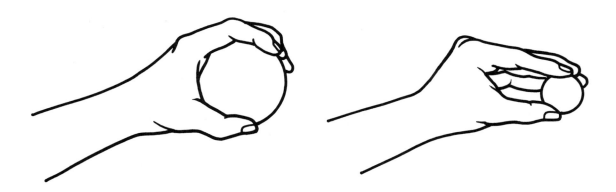

Fig. 12.2. Orange and Golf Ball Grips

Everyday Stretches

Arm Stretches

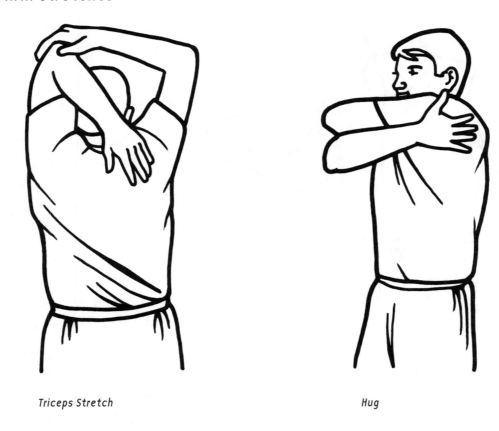

Triceps Stretch   Hug

Complete Arm Stretch

Fig. 12.3. Everyday Stretches. Hold each position for about 15-30 seconds, and repeat several times.

Back Stretches

Cat Stretch

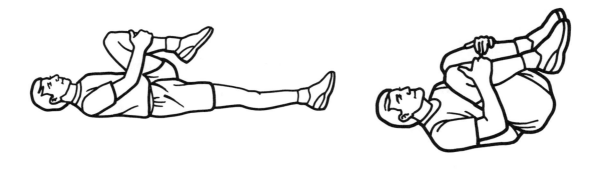

Lower Back Stretch

Fig. 12.3. Everyday Stretches. Hold each position for about 15-30 seconds, and repeat several times.

Medical Definitions

Bursa sac	The structure responsible for lubrication between and around tendons and bones.
Calcium deposit	The hardening of soft tissue, this usually occurs after repeated overuse or injury.
Carpals	Wrist bones.
Cartilage	The connecting tissue between bones. It is harder than ligament and softer than bone. It allows for smooth movement.
Fibrositis	The inflammation of connecting tissue, muscles, joints, tendons, or ligaments.
Itis	Inflamed.
Metacarpals	Palm bones.
Muscle	Tissue that produces movement through contractions. It functions best warmed up.
Neuritis	Inflammation of a nerve.
Radius	The thumb-side forearm bone.
Scar tissue	This forms after serious injury to replace lost tissue. Repeated injury widens the area of scar tissue causing permanent weakness.
Soft tissue	Anything but bone.
Tendon	The fibrous cord which attaches muscle to bone. It usually runs inside of a sheath.
Ulna	Pinky-side forearm bone.

CHAPTER 13

Considerations When Purchasing an Instrument

When someone tells me that they want to purchase an instrument, and what do I think, I always ask them the same two questions: "Do you like it?" and "Do you have the money?" These are, of course, simple, obvious questions, perhaps too simple and obvious. But a considerable amount of thoughtful consideration should be put into them before acting. Ultimately, these really are the only two questions you need answer.

When I ask if you like it, I am actually asking if it suit your needs. There are a number of factors to consider when answering this question.

Obviously, if you can afford an instrument, you can buy it, but should you? If you love an instrument, no amount of money is too much, is it?

How can you determine if an instrument suits your needs and what a fair price is? There are no definitive answers to these questions that will suit everyone, but there are some guidelines that all should consider.

In all cases, you must do your homework. The Internet and your local music stores are good places to start. Do some research to get a feel for what is available and how prices are running. Your most important action in this regard is to talk to as many other bass players as possible, trying to extract pertinent information from their experiences.

Does it suit your needs? Consider this question without thinking about the price. Try to answer these secondary questions first to determine your needs.

How experienced of a player are you? Are you a beginner? Are you sure you will be playing after five years? Are you playing gigs now? What don't you like about your present instrument? Are looks important? Do you require some bells and whistles? Are you looking for new or used? Is a brand name important? Have you considered a custom-made instrument? Do you know exactly what you want? What kind of music are you currently performing? Might you need several different instruments to meet your performance needs?

I could go on, but I think you might be getting the idea. You need to analyze your personal and professional requirements of an instrument. As you answer questions such as these, a clearer picture of what you think you need from an instrument should begin to appear to you. It is your answers that will ultimately teach you about the instrument that you need.

You need to play instruments that fit your criteria of what you think you want. Be sure that you do lots more homework here. Unless you are a beginner, you should play as many instruments as possible, so as to get a feel for all of the options available. Do not consider price at this point.

My advice to beginners, in this regard, is to seek counseling from a professional player of fifteen or more years, who has no vested interest in selling you a bass. A performer such as this can lend his experience to your research. Also, try to avoid a more complex bass for your first instrument, as beginners should be concerned with basic musical technique, not instrument types and options. Beginners have no concept of what they need from an instrument, and in most cases, a basic Fender, or the like, is the right choice in an electric. A used Kay or King plywood, or the like, is a fine choice for your first double bass. Many players form entire careers around instruments such as these, and you may be pleasantly surprised to find that you never need to purchase another bass.

The money issue is a little more cut-and-dried, but no one wants to overpay for something unnecessarily. If you can afford the instrument you have settled on, then go for it, but if you are short money, you may need to adjust your thinking somewhat. Comparison shop. Shop like you might for a car. If you are selling your present instrument, try to sell it outright rather than trading it in. This will help you to obtain top dollar. If you can afford to keep your present instrument, it may just come in handy as your career changes, matures, and sometimes circles.

With the tax laws as they are presently, your instrument purchase is a depreciation write-off, as long as you use it to generate income. This is, of course, the case for all of your musical equipment used to generate income, so you can consider a yearly savings in this manner, depending on your method of depreciation. The tax laws concerning depreciation and self-employed musicians are quite complicated, and you are well advised to research this subject thoroughly. The IRS has a number of free booklets related to this subject available to the public.

Prices of new instruments are not as negotiable as used ones, but you always stand a chance of lowering the price if you have done your research or can pit one seller against another. You need to be an informed consumer.

In general, buying a used instrument is a lot like buying stock. The price depends greatly on supply and demand. Naturally, prices will be higher in areas of large musical communities, and supplies will be low in out-of-the way places. But the world is connected via the Internet now, and for those of you savvy in its use, there are many fair deals to be obtained.

The prices of good electric basses can be as little as $300 or so and as much as $5,000 or more, so your research can pay off in lots of dollars to fill your hatchback's tank many times.

Double-bass prices can be a little more off-the-wall. Used plywoods needing some cosmetic or other minor work can often sell for under $1,000. Better quality plywoods can sell for up to $3,000 or more. Decent carved instruments usually start in the $3,000 range, and quality newer carved instruments are usually in the $10,000 to $15,000 range. If you think this is a lot of money, consider the fact that fine old instruments, like those used by the major orchestra players, are often valued from $20,000 to $50,000, or more!

If you are purchasing a carved double bass, it's a good idea to find out as much specific history related to the instrument as possible. Knowledge of previous repairs and owners, along with locations where the bass resided, can help you to anticipate future repair and maintenance needs.

Double bassists may also need to purchase a different bow. Of course, they come new or used, light and heavy, stiff and flexible, and as discussed earlier, are made from a number of materials. Again, I cannot tell exactly what you want to look for when shopping for a bow; only playing experience can teach you this. I do, however, believe that it is foolish to spend more than $200 to $500 on a bow unless you are a professional, working for a living, and know exactly what you want from it.

Many musical equipment catalogs offer a number of varying quality bows, which usually must be purchased sight unseen. Most often, you can send them back and try again, if you don't like them. This is a fine way to obtain a first bow or a fiberglass bow, but the experienced player will be best served to find a local source where many quality bows can be compared first hand.

Beginner to expert players can often make beautiful music for a lifetime with bows selling for under $500. If you do decide to purchase a more expensive bow, you can keep your old bow to use when your good bow is being rehaired. As with purchasing a bass, the most important thing you can do is to play as many bows as possible. Try not to consider the price as you first compare bows. You may just find that you like the least expensive one the best.

Do you like it, and do you have the money? It's really very simple, if you do your homework.

Resources

Bass Books

Appleman, Rich. *Reading Contemporary Electric Bass*. Boston: Berklee Press, 1983.

Appleman, Rich and John Repucci. *The Berklee Practice Method: Get Your Band Together*. Bass volume. Boston: Berklee Press, 2001.

Appleman, Rich and Joseph Viola. *Chord Studies for Electric Bass*. Boston: Berklee Press, 1981.

Bacon, T. and B. Moorhouse. *The Bass Book*. San Francisco: Miller Freeman Books, 1995.

Blasquiz, K. *The Fender Bass*. Milwaukee, WI: Hal Leonard Publishing Corp., 1991.

Brett, J. *Berlioz the Bear*. New York: G. P. Putnam's Sons, 1991.

Brun, P. *A History of the Double Bass*. Villeneuve d'ascq, France: P. Brun, 1989.

Elgar, R. *Looking at the Double Bass*. Princeton, NJ: Stephen W. Fillo, 1967.

Elgar, R. *More About the Double Bass*. Princeton, NJ: Stephen W. Fillo, 1963.

Elgar. R. *Introduction to the Double Bass*. Princeton, NJ: Stephen W. Fillo, 1960.

Morris, Danny. *Instant Bass*. Boston: Berklee Press, 2001.

Nanny, Edward. *Enseignment Complet de la Contrabasse a 4 et 5 cordes*. Paris: Éditions Musicales Andre Leduc, 1926.

Portnoi, H. *Creative Bass Technique.* Logan, UT: American String Teachers Association, 1978.

Santerre, Joe. *Rock Bass Lines.* Boston: Berklee Press, 2001.

Santerre, Joe. *Slap Bass Lines.* Boston: Berklee Press, 2001.

Simandl, F. *New Method for String Bass. Part 1 and Part 2.* New York: International Music Company, 1958.

Stanton, D. H. *The String (Double) Bass.* Evanston, IL: The Instrumentalist, 1965.

Zimmermann, F. *A Contemporary Concept of Bowing Technique for the Double Bass,* New York: MCA Music, 1966.

Zwaan, E. *Animal Magnetism for Musicians.* Amsterdam: EZ Tech Publication, 1988.

Bass Music and Studies*

J. S. Bach, J. S. *Six Suites for Violoncello Solo.* New York: Schirmer's Library of Music Classics, 1939.

Bellson, L. and Gil Breines. *A Modern Reading Text in 4/4.* Melville, NY: Belwin Mills Publishing Corp., 1963.

Kreutzer. *18 Studies.* New York: International Music Company.

Marcello Cello Sonatas, New York: International Music Company, 1951.

Nanny, Edward. *Nanny Virtuoso Etudes.* Paris: Éditions Musicales Andre Leduc, 1926.

Simandl, F. *30 Etude.* New York: International Music Co. 1956.

Slutsky, Allan. *Standing in the Shadows of Motown.* Wynnewood, PA: Dr. Licks Publication, 1989.

Storch and Hrabe, *57 Studies in Two Volumes,* New York: International Music Company.

Sturm. *110 Studies.* New York: International Music Company.

Vivaldi Cello Sonatas, New York: International Music Company, 1957.

Zimmermann, O. *Solos for the Double Bass Player.* New York: G. Schirmer, 1966.

* Much of this classical bass music literature is available from a number of different publishers.

General Music Books

Ammer, Christine. *The A to Z of Foreign Musical Terms*. Boston: ECS Publishing, 1989.

Backus, J. *The Acoustical Foundations of Music*. W. W. Norton & Co., 1977.

Fletcher and Rossing. *The Physics of Musical Instrument*. New York: Springer Verlag, 1998.

Green, Barry and W. Timothy Gallwey. *The Inner Game of Music*. New York: Double Day, 1986.

Hopkin, B. *Musical Instrument Design*. Tucson, AZ: See Sharp Press, 1996.

Jorgensen, O. *Tuning the Historical Temperaments by Ear*. Marquette, MI: The Northern Michigan University Press, 1977.

Levarie and Levy. *Tone: A Study in Musical Acoustics*. Greenwood Publishing Group, 1981.

Partch, H. *Genesis of Music*. Da Capo Printers, 1979.

Read, G. *Modern Rhythmic Notation*. Bloomington, IN: Indiana University Press, 1978.

Read, G. *Music Notation*. Boston: Allyn & Bacon Inc., 1964.

Reblitz, A. A. *Piano Servicing, Tuning & Rebuilding*. Vestal, NY: The Vestal Press, 1984.

Roederer, J. G. *Physics and Psychophysics of Music: An Introduction*. New York: Springer Verlag, 1995.

Slonimsky, N. *Thesaurus of Scales and Melodic Patterns*. New York: Charles Scribner's Sons, 1947.

Strobel, H. A. *Useful Measurements for Viol Makers*. Aumsville, OR: H. A. Strobel, 1990.

Other Books

Hanley and Belfus. *Medical Problems of the Performing Artist*. Philadelphia.

Herrigel, E. *Zen in the Art of Archery*. New York: Vintage Books, 1971.

Hoffman, M. and Dr. W. Southmayd. *Sports Health*. New York: Perigee Books, 1981.

Mangi, Dr. R., Dr. P. Jokl, and O. William Dayton. *Sports Fitness and Training*. New York: Pantheon Books, 1989.

McClain, E. *Myth of Invariance*. Shambale Press, Samuel Weiser, 1985.

Mingus, C. *Beneath the Underdog*. Vintage Books, 1991.

Norris, Dr. R., M.D. *The Musician's Survival Manual*. St. Louis, MO: The International Conference of Symphony and Opera Musicians, 1995.

Stone, Robert J. and Judith A. Stone. *Atlas of Skeletal Muscles*. Columbus, OH: McGraw Hill, 2000.

Thomas, L *The Lives of a Cell*. New York: Penguin USA, 1995.

Westcott, Dr. W. *Building Strength and Stamina*. Champagne, IL: Human Kinetics, 1996.

Yost, G. *Back Problems*. (Out of print)

About the Author

Since 1974, Greg Mooter has taught bass to well over a thousand students. He is an Associate Professor of Bass at Berklee College of Music, where he has taught since 1977. As an active studio and session player, Greg plays double bass, fretted electric, and fretless electric, frequenting jazz, rock, classical, pop, and theater music circles. He studied bass at Ohio State, the University of Cincinnati, and Berklee College of Music. His writing about playing bass has appeared in *Bass Player* magazine. Greg is also a certified personal trainer and teaches weight training at the South Shore YMCA in Quincy, MA.

Index

The Best Guitar Books from Berklee Press

BERKLEE BASIC GUITAR, PHASE 1 ▸ by William Leavitt
An ideal method for the beginning guitar student or guitar class. Technique and reading skills are developed through two, three and four-part ensemble arrangements of traditional and newly composed music. An introduction to chords is also included. A cassette demonstrates the ideal performance.
_____ 50449460 Book Only $7.95
_____ 50449462 Book/Cassette Pack $14.95

BERKLEE BASIC GUITAR, PHASE 2 ▸ by William Leavitt
A continuation of Phase I, this phase includes solo, two-part, and three-part ensemble arrangements of traditional and newly composed music for the beginning to intermediate student or class. Skills are developed through delightful arrangements of music by Bach, Foster, Leavitt, Schumann, and others.
_____ 50449470 Book Only $7.95

BERKLEE PRACTICE METHOD: GUITAR
GET YOUR BAND TOGETHER ▸ by Larry Baione
The first-ever method that teaches you how to play in a rock band! Improve your improvisation, timing, technique, and reading ability, and master your role in the groove. Become the great player that everyone wants to have in their band. Play along in a variety of styles with outstanding Berklee players on the CD, then jam with your own band.
_____ 50449426 Book/CD Pack $14.95

CLASSICAL STUDIES FOR PICK-STYLE GUITAR ▸ by William Leavitt
An outstanding collection of solos and duets for intermediate to advanced pick-style guitarists. Includes 21 pieces by Carcassi, Carulli, Sor, Bach, Paganini, Kreutzer and Clementi.
_____ 50449440 ....$9.95

COUNTRY GUITAR STYLES ▸ by Mike Ihde
For the guitarist who wants to learn the secrets of playing "country." Complete with detailed explanations, illustrations, notated examples, full-length solos, and a demonstration cassette tape. Styles and effects include country rhythm, single-note lead, pedal steel, bluegrass, fingerpicking, western, rockabilly, Memphis style, harmonics, string bending, electronic effects and more.
_____ 50449480 Book/Cassette Pack $14.95

JIM KELLY'S GUITAR WORKSHOP ▸ by Jim Kelly
_____ 00695230 Book/CD..$14.95
_____ 00320144 Video/Booklet..................................$19.95
_____ 00320168 DVD/Booklet.....................................$29.95

MORE GUITAR WORKSHOP ▸ by Jim Kelly
_____ 00695306 Book/CD..$14.95
_____ 00320158 Video/Booklet..................................$19.95

A MODERN METHOD FOR GUITAR 123 COMPLETE ▸ by William Leavitt
Used as the basic text by the Berklee College of Music guitar program, the Leavitt method has earned legions of loyal followers. Now you can have all three volumes in one convenient book at a great savings. A practical and comprehensive program for learning to play guitar, from beginner through advanced. Includes music fundamentals, scales, melodic studies, chord and arpeggio studies, intervals, chord construction and voicings, improvisation, and rhythm guitar technique.
_____ 50449468 ....$29.95
ALSO AVAILABLE IN SEPARATE VOLUMES:
VOLUME 1 ▸ _____ 50449404 Book/CD Pack $22.95
            _____ 50449402 Book/Cassette $22.95
            _____ 50449400 Book Only $14.95
VOLUME 2 ▸ _____ 50449412 Book/Cassette......$22.95
            _____ 50449410 Book.....................$14.95
VOLUME 3 ▸ _____ 50449420 Book Only $14.95

MELODIC RHYTHMS FOR GUITAR ▸ by William Leavitt
A thorough presentation of rhythms commonly found in contemporary music, including 68 harmonized melodies and 42 rhythm exercises. This is also an excellent source for duets, sight-reading and chord studies. The cassette features demonstration duets, as well as recorded rhythm section accompaniments so that the student can play melodies along with the tape.
_____ 50449450 Book Only $12.95

READING STUDIES FOR GUITAR ▸ by William Leavitt
A comprehensive collection of studies for improving reading and technical ability. Includes scales, arpeggios, written-out chords, and a variety of rhythms and time signatures. Positions 1 through 7 are covered in all keys. An important method for all guitarists who recognize the advantages of being able to sight-read.
_____ 50449490 ....$12.95

ADVANCED READING STUDIES FOR GUITAR ▸ by William Leavitt
For the guitarist who wants to improve reading ability in positions 8 through 12, 112 pages of progressive studies written especially for the guitar, in all keys, and consisting of scales, arpeggios, intervals, and notated chords in various time signatures. A special section of multi-position studies is included. An important method for all guitarists who want to learn the entire fingerboard.
_____ 50449500 ....$12.95

ROCK GUITAR STYLES ▸ by Mike Ihde
This popular hands-on book will teach the modern guitarist how to play lead and rhythm guitar. Styles include heavy metal, hard rock, new wave, blues, jazz-rock, funk and more. Electronic equipment is also discussed. Five additional arrangements for lead guitar, rhythm guitar, bass and drums are included. Many music examples and a demonstration cassette make this the player's method of choice. 33-minute audio accompaniment.
_____ 50449520 Book/Cassette Pack $14.95

As Serious About Music As You Are.

For more information about Berklee Press
or Berklee College of Music, contact us:
1140 Boylston Street▸ Boston, MA 02215-3693 ▸ 617-747-2146
www.berkleepress.com

Visit your local music dealer or bookstore,
or go to www.berkleepress.com
Prices and availability subject to change without notice.

DISTRIBUTED BY

0402

More Fine Publications from Berklee Press

As Serious About Music As You Are.

GUITAR

THE GUITARIST'S GUIDE TO COMPOSING AND IMPROVISING
► by Jon Damian
50449497 Book/CD............$24.95

BERKLEE BASIC GUITAR
► by William Leavitt
Phase 1
50449462 Book/Cassette $14.95
50449460 Book Only $7.95
Phase 2
50449470 Book Only $7.95

CLASSICAL STUDIES FOR PICK-STYLE GUITAR ► by William Leavitt
50449440 Book............$9.95

A MODERN METHOD FOR GUITAR 123 COMPLETE
► by William Leavitt
50449468 Book............$29.95
Also available in separate volumes:
Volume 1: Beginner
50449404 Book/CD............$22.95
50449400 Book Only $14.95
Volume 2: Intermediate
50449412 Book/Cassette $22.95
50449410 Book Only $14.95
Volume 3: Advanced
50449420 Book............$14.95

MELODIC RHYTHMS FOR GUITAR
► by William Leavitt
50449450 Book............$14.95

READING CONTEMPORARY GUITAR RHYTHMS ► by M. T. Szymczak
50449530 Book............$10.95

READING STUDIES FOR GUITAR
► by William Leavitt
50449490 Book............$14.95

ADVANCED READING STUDIES FOR GUITAR
► by William Leavitt
50449500 Book............$14.95

JIM KELLY GUITAR WORKSHOP SERIES

JIM KELLY'S GUITAR WORKSHOP
00695230 Book/CD............$14.95
00320144 Video/booklet $19.95
00320168 DVD/booklet $29.95

MORE GUITAR WORKSHOP
► by Jim Kelly
00695306 Book/CD............$14.95
00320158 Video/booklet $19.95

BASS

CHORD STUDIES FOR ELECTRIC BASS
► by Rich Appleman
50449750 Book............$14.95

INSTANT BASS ► by Danny Morris
50449502 Book/CD............$14.95

READING CONTEMPORARY ELECTRIC BASS
► by Rich Appleman
50449770 Book............$14.95

ROCK BASS LINES
► by Joe Santerre
50449478 Book/CD............$19.95

SLAP BASS LINES
► by Joe Santerre
50449508 Book/CD............$19.95

KEYBOARD

A MODERN METHOD FOR KEYBOARD
► by James Progris
50449620 Vol. 1: Beginner $14.95
50449630 Vol. 2: Intermediate $14.95
50449640 Vol. 3: Advanced $14.95

DRUM SET

BEYOND THE BACKBEAT
► by Larry Finn
50449447 Book/CD............$19.95

DRUM SET WARM-UPS
► by Rod Morgenstein
50449465 Book............$12.95

MASTERING THE ART OF BRUSHES
► by Jon Hazilla
50449459 Book/CD............$19.95

THE READING DRUMMER
► by Dave Vose
50449458 Book............$9.95

SAXOPHONE

CREATIVE READING STUDIES FOR SAXOPHONE ► by Joseph Viola
50449870 Book............$14.95

TECHNIQUE OF THE SAXOPHONE
► by Joseph Viola
50449820 Volume 1: Scale Studies $14.95
50449830 Volume 2: Chord Studies $14.95
50449840 Volume 3: Rhythm Studies $14.95

TOOLS FOR DJs

**TURNTABLE TECHNIQUE:
THE ART OF THE DJ**
► by Stephen Webber
50449482 Book/2-Record Set $34.95

TURNTABLE BASICS ► by Stephen Webber
50449514 Book $9.95

VITAL VINYL, VOLUMES 1-5
► by Stephen Webber
12" records
50449491 Volume 1: Needle Juice $15.95
50449492 Volume 2: Turntablist's Toolkit........$15.95
50449493 Volume 3: Rockin' the House $15.95
50449494 Volume 4: Beat Bomb $15.95
50449495 Volume 5: Tech Tools for DJs $15.95

TOOLS FOR DJs SUPERPACK
► by Stephen Webber
50449529 Includes Turntable Technique book/2-record
set and all 5 Vital Vinyl records (a $115 value!) ..$99.95

BERKLEE PRACTICE METHOD

Get Your Band Together

BASS ► by Rich Appleman and John Repucci
50449427 Book/CD....................................$14.95

DRUM SET ► by Ron Savage and
Casey Scheuerell
50449429 Book/CD....................................$14.95

GUITAR ► by Larry Baione
50449426 Book/CD....................................$14.95

KEYBOARD ► by Russell Hoffmann and
Paul Schmeling
50449428 Book/CD....................................$14.95

ALTO SAX ► by Jim Odgren and Bill Pierce
50449437 Book/CD....................................$14.95

TENOR SAX ► by Jim Odgren and Bill Pierce
50449431 Book/CD....................................$14.95

TROMBONE ► by Jeff Galindo
50449433 Book/CD....................................$14.95

TRUMPET ► by Tiger Okoshi and Charles
Lewis
50449432 Book/CD....................................$14.95

BERKLEE INSTANT SERIES

BASS ► by Danny Morris
50449502 Book/CD....................................$14.95

DRUM SET ► by Ron Savage
50449513 Book/CD....................................$14.95

GUITAR ► by Tomo Fujita
50449522 Book/CD....................................$14.95

KEYBOARD ► by Paul Schmeling and
Dave Limina
50449525 Book/CD....................................$14.95

IMPROVISATION SERIES

BLUES IMPROVISATION COMPLETE ►
by Jeff Harrington ► Book/CD Packs
50449486 Bb Instruments.............................$19.95
50449488 C Bass Instruments $19.95
50449425 C Treble Instruments $19.95
50449487 Eb Instruments $19.95

A GUIDE TO JAZZ IMPROVISATION
► by John LaPorta ► Book/CD Packs
50449439 C Instruments $16.95
50449441 Bb Instruments.............................$16.95
50449442 Eb Instruments $16.95
50449443 Bass Clef $16.95

MUSIC TECHNOLOGY

ARRANGING IN THE DIGITAL WORLD
► by Corey Allen
50449415 Book/GM disk $19.95

**FINALE: AN EASY GUIDE TO MUSIC
NOTATION** ► by Thomas E. Rudolph and
Vincent A. Leonard, Jr.
50449501 Book/CD-ROM $59.95

**PRODUCING IN THE HOME STUDIO
WITH PRO TOOLS** ► by David Franz
50449526 Book/CD-ROM $34.95

RECORDING IN THE DIGITAL WORLD
► by Thomas E. Rudolph and
Vincent A. Leonard, Jr.
50449472 Book $29.95

MUSIC BUSINESS

**HOW TO GET A JOB IN THE MUSIC &
RECORDING INDUSTRY**
► by Keith Hatschek
50449505 Book $24.95

THE SELF-PROMOTING MUSICAN
► by Peter Spellman
50449423 Book $24.95

THE MUSICIAN'S INTERNET
► by Peter Spellman
50449527 Book $24.95

REFERENCE

COMPLETE GUIDE TO FILM SCORING
► by Richard Davis
50449417 Book $24.95

THE CONTEMPORARY SINGER
► by Anne Peckham
50449438 Book/CD....................................$24.95

ESSENTIAL EAR TRAINING
► by Steve Prosser
50449421 Book $14.95

MODERN JAZZ VOICINGS ► by Ted
Pease and Ken Pullig
50449485 Book/CD....................................$24.95

**THE NEW MUSIC THERAPIST'S
HANDBOOK, SECOND EDITION**
► by Suzanne B. Hanser
50449424 Book $29.95

POP CULTURE

INSIDE THE HITS
► by Wayne Wadhams
50449476 Book $29.95

**MASTERS OF MUSIC:
CONVERSATIONS WITH
BERKLEE GREATS** ► by Mark Small and
Andrew Taylor
50449422 Book $24.95

SONGWRITING

MELODY IN SONGWRITING
► by Jack Perricone
50449419 Book $19.95

MUSIC NOTATION ► by Mark McGrain
50449399 Book $19.95

**SONGWRITING: ESSENTIAL GUIDE
TO LYRIC FORM AND STRUCTURE**
► by Pat Pattison
50481582 Book $14.95

**SONGWRITING: ESSENTIAL GUIDE
TO RHYMING** ► by Pat Pattison
50481583 Book $14.95

Bass Books
from Berklee Press

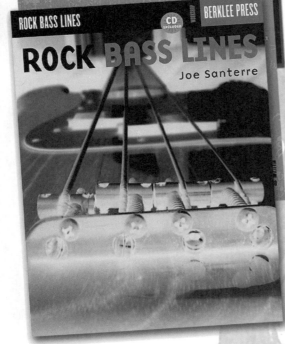